Nelson Thornes Shake

Macbeth

Nelson Thornes Shakespeare

Macbeth

Volume editor: **Dinah Jurksaitis**

Series editors: **Duncan Beal and Dinah Jurksaitis**

Series consultant: **Peter Thomas**

Published in 2003 by:
Nelson Thornes Ltd
Delta Place
27 Bath Road
CHELTENHAM
GL53 7TH
United Kingdom

06 07 08 09/ 10 9 8 7 6 5 4 3 2

A catalogue record for this book is available from the British Library

ISBN 0 7487 6955 2

Illustrations by Peters and Zabranski

Page make-up by Tech-Set

Printed and bound in Spain by Graphycems

Acknowledgements
Bridgeman Art Library/The Hamburg Kunsthalle, Germany: p100; Bridgeman Art Library/The Louvre, Paris: p116; Zoe Dominic: p82; Fortean Picture Library: p84; Mary Evans Picture Library: p3 (both), p12, p72, p94; Photostage/Donald Cooper: P46; V&A Picture Library/Theatre Museum: p24, p54

Contents

Preface

The very name *Shakespeare* can overwhelm: so many associations with culture and history. We hope you will approach the plays with curiosity and a willingness to embrace the strangeness of Shakespeare's world: those quaint ways, weapons and words!

Our aim in the **Nelson Thornes Shakespeare** series is to provide a bridge between Shakespeare's world, and our own. For all the differences between the two worlds it is intriguing to find so many similarities: parents and children; power games; loyalty and treachery; prejudice; love and hate; fantasy and reality; comedy and horror; the extremes of human behaviour. It is oddly moving to find that the concerns of the human race have not changed so much over the centuries, and that Shakespeare's themes are modern and recognisable.

The unfamiliarity of the language is best regarded not as a barrier, but as a source of interest. On the left-hand pages we have not only explained unfamiliar words, but have also drawn attention to aspects of wordplay, imagery and verse. The left-hand pages also have reminders that this is a piece of theatre, written to be performed and experienced visually. The **performance features** boxes invite you to consider such questions as: *How might this character react? What actions might be appropriate here? Try reading/acting this section in this way...* You are not fed one interpretation; you make the decisions.

To help you place individual scenes in the context of the whole play there is a **comparison feature** at the end of each scene: *Where else have we seen characters behaving like this? How do events in this scene parallel events two scenes back?* A brief **scene summary** brings together the main developments within that scene.

At the beginning of the play there are some **introductory essays** on background topics. They highlight aspects of Shakespeare's world which show a different outlook to our own: *How did they conduct courtship in his day? How has the status of the monarchy changed? What about their view of magic and the supernatural?*

A separate **Teacher Resource Book** contains material which will help deepen your understanding of the play. There are **worksheets** on individual scenes – valuable if you have missed any of the class study. They will also provide a good background which will help you demonstrate your knowledge in coursework essays. To this end, the book also contains some **Coursework Assignment essay titles** and hints on how to tackle them. The play and resource book together provide enough support to allow you to study independently, and to select the assignment you want to do, rather than all working together as a class.

Our aim is that you finish the play enthused and intrigued, and eager to explore more of Shakespeare's works. We hope you will begin to see that although ideally the plays are experienced in performance, there is also a place for reading together and discussing as a class, or for simply reading them privately to yourself.

Foreword

Who bothers to read introductions, especially introductions to plays by Shakespeare?

Well, you do, obviously, and that's a good start if you want to get more from your literature study. Reading this Foreword will help you to get more from Shakespeare's writing and from the accompanying material provided with the play.

Shakespeare – the great adapter

Shakespeare is regarded as a great writer but not because he was an original inventor of stories. His plays are nearly all adaptations of stories he found in books, or in history – or in somebody else's play. His originality came from the way he used this material. He changed his sources to suit himself and his audiences and was never afraid to change the facts if they didn't suit him.

The best way of understanding what Shakespeare thought valuable in a story is to look at the way he altered what he found.

The **Introductory essays** show how he changed characters or time-scales to enhance the dramatic effect or to suit a small cast of actors.

Shakespeare – the great realist

What Shakespeare added to his source material was his insight into people and society. He understood what makes people tick and what makes society hold together or fall apart. He showed how people behave – and why – by showing their motives and their reactions to experiences such as love, loss, dreams, fears, threats and doubts. These have not changed, even if we think science and technology make us different from people in Shakespeare's day. He was also realistic. He avoided stereotypes, preferring to show people as a complex mixture of changing emotions.

When you use the character sheets provided by your teacher, you will see this realism in action. His characters behave differently in different circumstances, and they change over time – just as we do in real life.

Shakespeare – the language magician

Shakespeare's cleverness with language is not just his ability to write beautiful poetry. He also wrote amusing dialogue, common slang, rude insults and the thoughts of people under pressure. He wrote script that uses the sounds of words to convey emotion, and the associations of words to create vivid images in our heads.

When you use the glossary notes you will see how his language expresses ugliness, hatred, suspicion, doubt and fear as well as happiness, beauty and joy.

Shakespeare – the theatrical innovator

Theatre before Shakespeare was different from today. Ordinary people enjoyed songs and simple shows, and educated people – the minority – enjoyed stories from Latin and Greek. Moral and religious drama taught right and wrong and there were spectacular masques full of music and dance for the audience to join in. Shakespeare put many of these elements together, so most people could expect something to appeal to them. He was a comprehensive writer for a comprehensive audience, writing to please the educated and the uneducated. He was the first to put realistic people from every walk of life on stage – not just kings and generals, but characters who talked and behaved like the ordinary folk in the audience. He was less interested in right and wrong than in the comedy or tragedy of what people actually do. *Only Fools and Horses*, and *EastEnders*, are dramas which follow a trend started by Shakespeare over four hundred years ago. He managed this in theatres which lacked lighting, sound amplification, scene changes, curtains or a large cast of actors.

The performance features accompanying the play text will help to show you how Shakespeare's stagecraft is used to best dramatic effect.

Whether you are studying for GCSE or AS, the examination is designed to test your ability to respond to the following:
1 Shakespeare's ideas and themes
2 Shakespeare's use of language
3 Shakespeare's skill in writing for stage performance
4 The social, cultural and historical aspects of his plays
5 Different interpretations of the plays.

1a. Showing personalities (ideas and themes)
Shakespeare thought drama should do more than preach simple moral lessons. He thought it should show life as it was, daft and serious, joyful and painful. He didn't believe in simple versions of good and evil, heroes and villains. He thought most heroes had unpleasant parts to their nature, just as most villains had good parts. This is why he showed people as a mixture. In *Hamlet*, he wrote that the dramatist should **hold a mirror up to nature**, so that all of us can see ourselves reflected. As he picks on the parts of human behaviour that don't change (fear, jealousy, doubt, self-pity), his characters remind us of people we know today – and of ourselves – not just people who lived a long time ago. This is because Shakespeare shows us more than his characters' status in life. He knew that beneath the robes or the crown there is a heart the same as any tradesman's or poor person's. He knew that nobody in real life is perfect – so he didn't put perfect characters on his stage.

Macbeth is brave, respected and a successful soldier. Others admire him and he seems to have everything. He is also ambitious – and this ambition first gains him what he wants, then loses him everything. In the course of the play Shakespeare shows him heroic, pathetic, despicable and despairing.

1b. Showing what society was/is like (ideas and themes)

In *Hamlet*, Shakespeare declared that drama should show the **form and pressure of the age**', meaning the structure of the times we live in and the pressures and influences it creates.

Elizabethan England had known great conflict and turmoil through civil unrest and was also always under threat from other countries (Shakespeare was 20 at the time of the Spanish Armada). It was also a nation changing from the old ways of country living. London and other cities were growing, and voyagers were exploring other lands. New trades were developing, and plague and disease spread quickly in crowded parts of the cities. Most people were superstitious, but science was beginning to make its mark. People still generally believed in the Divine Right of Kings, but they were beginning to think that bad kings may be removed for the country's good. One such example was Charles I who was executed only 33 years after Shakespeare's death.

In *Macbeth*, witchcraft represents the old ways and the old forces of kingship and loyalty, and the effects of trying to establish a dictator's hold on the country. Shakespeare shows how even brutal repression produces resistance.

2. Shakespeare's use of the English language (sound and image)

Shakespeare wrote the speech of uneducated servants and traders but he could also write great speeches using rhetoric. Whether it is a dim-witted inn-servant called Francis in *Henry IV Part One*, or a subtle political operator like Mark Antony in *Julius Caesar*, Shakespeare finds words to make them sound and seem convincing.

In *Macbeth*, Shakespeare reproduces the hushed, intense whispering of desperate thoughts in Macbeth's muttered, **If it were done, when 'tis done, then 'twere well it were done quickly** and **with his surcease, success.**

3a. Writing for a mixed audience (writing for stage performance)

As a popular dramatist who made his money by appealing to the widest range of people, Shakespeare knew that some of his audience would be literate, and some not. So he made sure that there was something for everybody – something clever and something vulgar, something comic and something tragic.

Macbeth gives its audiences brutal murders and eerie scenes of witches' chants and dances, as well as illusions of kings and the trick effects of a walking forest. Just when the horror is about to overwhelm the audience, Shakespeare introduces the Porter with his topical jokes and rude references to sex and drinking.

3b. Shakespeare's craft (writing for stage performance)

Shakespeare worked with very basic stage technology but, as a former actor, he knew how to give his actors the guidance they needed. His scripts use embedded prompts, either to actors, or to the audience, so that he did not have to write stage directions for his actors. If an actor says, **Put your cap to its proper purpose**, it is a cue to another actor to be using his hat for fancy gestures, rather than wearing it on his head. If an actor comes on stage and says, **So this is the forest of Arden**, we know where the scene is set, without expensive props and scenery.

In *Macbeth*, when things are going from bad to worse, Shakespeare writes lines that have the actor playing Macbeth whirl around in frenzied indecision as he can't keep his thoughts on any subject for long: **Doctor, my thanes flee from me... Come sir, dispatch!**

4. Social, cultural and historical aspects

There are two ways of approaching this. One way is to look at what the plays reveal for us about life in Shakespeare's time – and how it is different from today. The other is to look at what the plays reveal for us about life in Shakespeare's time – and how it is the same today.

If you learn from *Macbeth* that years ago a man could change from being loyal and honourable into someone brutal and deceitful just for ambition, you can ask yourself if things are different in the 21st century.

5. Alternative interpretations

You can look at Shakespeare's play in its own time and in ours and sometimes see differences, and sometimes see similarities. Your literature study expects you to understand how Shakespeare can be interpreted by different people in different eras and in different places. It's important to have your own view of how the plays should be performed.

The notes and commentary throughout this edition will help you to form your own interpretation, and to understand how others might interpret differently. Look especially at references to how different stage and film productions have taken different approaches to the script that Shakespeare wrote.

Enjoy Shakespeare's play! It's your play, too!

Peter Thomas

Introductory essays

Witches

In 16th- and 17th-century Britain, people feared and suspected witches and their powers. In Chelmsford there was a series of famous trials and hangings for witchcraft from 1566 to 1589, and pamphlets were circulated with details and illustrations of witches and their alleged deeds.

James I was fascinated by witches and wrote a book entitled *Daemonologie* (1597) that reinforced the views commonly held at that time. In the North Berwick witch trials of 1590–2, witches said they had plotted, and brought about, storms at sea when James went to Denmark to collect his new bride. James called them 'extreme lyars' until one of them repeated the conversation he had had with his wife, Anne, on their wedding night. He allowed them to be tortured and executed. His book supported the view that there were more women witches than men because women are weak and predisposed to evil. In 1604 a Witchcraft Act was introduced in England, with tough penalties. However, James was conscious that witchcraft was a difficult crime to prove and fewer than 40 people were executed for it in the 22 years of his reign.

Macbeth is full of echoes of popularly held ideas at the time about witches.

- They flew on dark, filthy or foggy air, which held them up (see the opening scene). Their activities, such as collecting ingredients for their cauldrons, were usually carried out at night. Yew was gathered during an eclipse of the moon.
- Familiars, ie witches' assistants sent to bewitch people, were cats, toads, owls, mice, dogs. Like any household pet they were given names. A 16th-century Essex witch had three mice called Littleman, Prettyman and Daynty. Familiars were well looked after, often dressed, and taught to dance! One woman in the Chelmsford trials had a cat called Sathan (Macbeth's servant is Seyton).
- Witches could tie winds in knots, in a rope or a handkerchief, and sell them to sailors. Untie one knot and you get a gentle wind; two and it is a strong wind; three and it is a tempest (the story about the sailor).
- Three is an important number. Illustrations often show a group of three witches.
- Spell chants are inverted prayers. They use ritual movements and words, and also special objects (like the thumb).
- The cauldron can be seen as the evil opposite of the chalice of the Holy Grail and communion.
- People were often thought to be bewitched by food and drink (Lady Macbeth's potions to the guards).
- Witches and their familiars could change shape (when Macbeth sees the ghost he would prefer it to come in another shape – for example, like the Hyrcan tiger).

- Witches cut off parts from unconsecrated dead bodies to use for spells. They take a thumb from a shipwrecked sailor, whose body is unburied; a finger from a prostitute's unwanted baby, strangled at birth and therefore not baptised. The Turk, the Tartar and the Jew are all non-Christians and therefore are not baptised. The witches use their nose, lips and liver. The hanged murderer's body is unburied and they use the grease from it. Soldiers killed in battle are not buried, so the witches go to Scotland's battle to pick up some body parts! James I added to the witchcraft laws a clause that declared the death penalty for using body parts.

- Hecate was a goddess of fertility, moon, night and ghosts and caused nightmares and insanity. She wore a necklace of testicles and her hair was snakes (Lady Macbeth mocks her husband's masculinity and refers to snakes).

- The 'hand of glory' was a charm especially used in burglaries. It was the severed hand, specially preserved, of a hanged murderer. The body fat was used with a wick to create candles, which were lit to keep the occupants of the house in a deep sleep while the theft took place. John Fian, tortured as a witch in Scotland in 1590, used a 'hand of glory' to break into a church and perform a service to the Devil. Once the flame is lit, it can only be put out by milk (hands are highlighted in the murder of Duncan; Macbeth's and Lady Macbeth's hands cannot be cleaned, and milk is turned to gall).

- Tortures used to extract confessions from suspected witches included forced walking and sleep deprivation (Lady Macbeth sleepwalks and Macbeth has murdered sleep).

- There was a pining spell. Those people who were bewitched pined away, or their bodies shrank up, until they died (the pilot pines and Macbeth threatens his servant with a shrinking famine in Act 5).

Stages of possession by evil spirits

- Faulty judgement and immoral choices (Macbeth decides to kill Duncan).
- The person allows him or herself to be possessed (Macbeth knows that what he is doing is wrong).
- Final possession (Macbeth returns to the witches for more guidance).

Some signs of possession

- Superhuman strength, often accompanied by fits and convulsions (the banquet scene).
- Having knowledge of the future and other secret information (Macbeth learns about the future from the witches).
- Ignorance of the possessed person about his fits and strange behaviours (Macbeth is not aware, like Lady Macbeth is, of his strange behaviour at the banquet).
- Being tired of living and therefore near to suicide (**'Tomorrow and tomorrow'**) *(Act 5 Scene 5, line 19)*.

The Hand of Glory (from Guiley's *The Encyclopedia of Witches and Witchcraft*).

Hand of an executed criminal used by a robber who thinks it makes him invisible.

The banquet

The banquet, eating and drinking together in a trusting community, is a very important aspect in the play. Food and drink is an important symbol in many religions (for example, the Passover in Judaism; Eid, at the end of Ramadan, in Islam) and is a confirmation of social togetherness in many cultures (for example, weddings, funerals, national days, anniversaries).

In the Christian religion, The Last Supper is when Jesus broke bread and drank wine with his disciples just before being betrayed by Judas and then crucified. Communion, when Christians eat bread and drink wine at the altar, commemorates this and symbolises being together and with God.

In Act 1 Scene 7, Macbeth has left the table where Duncan is feasting with the other thanes. He speaks of his plan to murder Duncan,

> ' 'twere well / It were done quickly,'

and then of a

> **'poisoned chalice'**

Lady Macbeth, when she comes out, says the king

> **'has almost supped'.**

The quotation below, from St John 13 in the Bible, describes the moment when Judas leaves the table to betray Jesus. There are similarities.

'And supper being ended, the devil having now put into the heart of Judas Iscariot, Simon's son, to betray him;' *(verse 2)*

'Then Jesus said unto him, That thou doest , do quickly.' *(verse 27)*

'He then ... went immediately out: and it was night.' *(verse 30)*

In Act 4 Scene 1, the witches prepare a cauldron for their charm that will produce

'Double, double toil and trouble'

from a sort of casserole of devilish ingredients. The cauldron is the evil opposite of the chalice. They have their own community as we see when Hecate, their leader joins them with other witches.

At the banquet, Act 3 Scene 4, Macbeth cannot sit down at the table with the other thanes. Before he goes into the banquet, in Scene 2, he mentions Hecate, the witches' goddess, and declares

'there shall be done / A deed of dreadful note'

He is now part of their other community. The ghost of Banquo (whose name is significant) pushes Macbeth from his stool. Lady Macbeth says her husband has

'broke the good meeting with ... disorder'

She means that he has spoilt the party by throwing a tantrum; but he has also broken peace and trust in his country by his murders. He can no longer join in the meal.

The Gunpowder Plot and equivocation

- In 1603 James I became King of England and Scotland.
- Many Catholics, and Protestants also, felt, possibly with reason, that he was unfair to them.
- In November 1605 the Gunpowder Plot was uncovered; Guy Fawkes was found.
- In 1606 Father Garnet (the equivocator) was tried and hanged as a plotter.
- Macbeth was probably written between 1603 and 1606.

The discovery of the Gunpowder Plot on 5 November 1605, when plotters attempted to blow up the Houses of Parliament, King James I, the Queen, the young heir, Prince Henry and all the Members of Parliament, has long been celebrated in England as Bonfire Night. Guy Fawkes was discovered in the cellar, with twenty barrels of explosives. A warning clue was sent in a letter, which said that parliament would receive a 'blow' on 5 November. The king rightly guessed that 'blow' meant 'to blow up' and this was interpreted as God saving him from the plotters. Many Catholics, who had reason for grievances at that time, were connected with the plot, including Robert Catesby, who was from Warwickshire, like Shakespeare, and whom Shakespeare knew. There were so many conspirators from Warwickshire that a special bench of jurors met at Stratford-upon-Avon in 1606 to investigate the plot.

One of the conspirators was a man called Digby, who was a close friend of King James. Betrayal by a trusted friend is shown in *Macbeth*. The plotters were very rapidly surrounded on 7 November in Holbeach House. Secret plotting, informing and betrayal were common at this dangerous time. Some historians believe that the Catholics were framed. Certainly, different types of Christianity could not be practised freely. However, there is no avoiding the fact that there was a multi-murderous plot.

The inferno that was being planned in the cellar under the Houses of Parliament made people think of the terrible fires of Hell. First, it was underground. Furthermore, the conspirators were plotting a treasonous murder. Plotters have existed in English history before, so why has this one been celebrated with such popularity? Could it be because of the name, Guy Fawkes? It sounds today like 'forks'. The Devil has a pitchfork and forked horns on his head, and the devil serpent, in the Garden of Eden, has a forked (double) tongue! In 1606, Fawkes was also pronounced 'fox', which led to many word games.

In the spring and summer of 1606 equivocation was a burning topic. According to reports from the time, Father Garnet, a Catholic priest accused of being part of the plot, had persistently denied his involvement. Later, when it was proved that he had purposely misled his accusers, he called his action 'equivocation'. Edmund Campion, a priest who came to England pretending to be a farmer in order to try to re-convert the English to Catholicism (and later executed as a spy in 1581), would have supported the view that equivocation for a good purpose was acceptable. This is an interesting topic for debate, and indeed it was widely discussed at the time. Garnet also said that as long as his accusers had no proof against him, he was not bound to accuse himself. Apparently, he consoled himself with drink and was also known as 'the farmer' (both these details are included in the Porter's speech). In May 1606, he was hanged.

People were fascinated and horrified. What is equivocation and what can it lead to?

Well, what is it? The word comes from the Latin, 'equal speaking'. The dictionary definition is 'To use ambiguous words or expressions in order to mislead'. The witches equivocate with Macbeth and he equivocates with the thanes. (For a detailed explanation and activities, see the Teacher Resource Book.)

Holinshed's *Chronicles of Scotland* (1587)

Holinshed wrote about England and Scotland, basing his histories loosely on the events of the past and supporting the Tudor dynasty as the rightful and best monarchs for England. He showed that James I was descended from Banquo, and Shakespeare followed this when he presented the witches' apparition of the eight kings in the line, the last one representing James I.

T

Shakespeare's play follows very closely the history of Macbeth, and of other people living in 11th-century Scotland, as Holinshed described them. The stories, however, of what happened, the words people used, details of how people felt, and what sort of people they were, are very graphically told in the chronicle. Shakespeare turned these into a play and kept much of the lively detail from this version of the history. He used the witches' words, to Macbeth and Banquo, as written by Holinshed. Some of the language of the stories clearly gave him the inspiration for images and symbols in the play (sleep and cup). The vivid details of the murder come from the history of a man called Donwald. Shakespeare was after all writing a play. It did not have to be exactly as this history described it and Holinshed also had been free with his version of events. Here is an edited version of these stories. The original account is in italics.

A captaine of the castell called Donwald had a grudge against a King Duff. The king *oftentimes used to lodge in his house without anie gard about him.* Donwald, *kindled in wrath by the words of his wife, determined to follow her advise in the execution of so heinous an act,* a murder. The king went to bed and *two of his chamberlains ... came forth again and then fell to banketting with Donwald and his wife ... who had prepared ... sundrie sorts of drinks ... till asleep they were so fast, that a man might have removed the chamber over them.*

In this story, Donwald employed four men to *cut his throte and they carried forth the dead body into the fields.* Donwald later *slue the chamberlains as guiltie of that heinous murther and then like a mad man running to and fro, he ransacked everie corner.* Then *some of the lords began to mislike the matter, and to smell foorth shrewd tokens, that he should not be altogether cleare himselfe. But ... they doubted to utter what they thought.* After this, *monstrous sights were seene ... : horsses ... did eate their owne flesh ... There was a sparhawke also strangled by an owle.*

Later, a King Kenneth killed his nephew and afterwards *to himselfe he seemed most unhappie, as he could not but still live in continuall feare. He heard a voice of vengeance and then passed the night without anie sleepe comming in his eies.*

Duncan became king. He was related to a thane of Glammis, *Makbeth, a valiant gentleman, and one that if he had not been somewhat cruell of nature, might have been thought most worthie of the governement of a realme ...* There was another thane, *Banquho ... , of whom the house of the Stewards is descended* (the forefather of Shakespeare's King James I). A traitor, Makdowald, led rebels with Kerns and Gallowglasses from the Western Isles, and Macbeth and Banquo beat them. Sweno invaded Scotland from Norway and was likewise beaten by the two heroes.

Holinshed tells the entire story of the witches; meeting Macbeth and Banquo and foretelling their futures. Shakespeare used much of Holinshed's detail here including the witches' words: *All haile Makbeth, thane of Glammis, Haile Makbeth thane of Cawdor, All haile Makbeth that hereafter shalt be king of Scotland,* and Holinshed's version of Banquo's words, *What manner of women are you?*

They said that Macbeth would reign, have an unlucky end and no children to follow him and that Banquo would not reign at all *but of thee those shall be borne which shall govern the Scotish kingdom by long order of continuall descent.* The witches vanished. Malcolm, Duncan's son, was made Prince of Cumberland. *Makbeth [was] sore troubled herewith. He considered murder and speciallie his wife lay sore upon him ... as she was verie ambitious.*

Macbeth asked for, and got, Banquo's help to kill the king. Shakespeare changed this part to avoid offending James I, who was descended from Banquo.

Macbeth reigned and for ten years *set his whole intention to mainteine iustice, and to punish all enormities and abuses, which had chanced through the feeble and slouthfull administration of Duncane.*

But things changed *For the pricke of conscience ... caused him ever to feare, least he should be served of the same cup, as he had ministred to his predecessor.* He arranged the killing of Banquo at a distance from the palace and Fleance escaped. Macbeth had a new castle built and the thanes were told to bring men and come themselves to help. Macduff did not come and Macbeth was angry. He feared Macduff even though he believed the witches, who said *that he should never be slaine with man borne of anie woman, nor vanquished till the wood of Bernane came to the castell of Dunsinane.* He sent men to kill Macduff's wife and children. It is then recorded how Macduff spoke with Malcolm in England, and was tested by him exactly as Shakespeare presented it. When his army arrived in Scotland, Malcolm *commanded everie man to get a bough of some tree.* In the battle, Macduff told Macbeth how he was not born normally from his mother but *ripped out of her womb.* He then killed Macbeth. He had ruled for 17 years. Malcolm became king and gave the title of earl to any thane who had helped him. (A fuller version of Holinshed's account can be found in the Arden Shakespeare critical edition.)

There are other details that Shakespeare added to the play, but Holinshed's history of a man who lived 550 years before Shakespeare wrote about him, provided both the backbone to the story and many dramatic points.

It is interesting to wonder what history stories from 550 years ago could be used today and brought to life as dramas.

Listening to Shakespeare's play

Shakespeare's audiences referred to going to 'hear' a play. We say we are going to 'see' a play. This does not mean that the plays then were not spectacles: they were often enormously visual and elaborate. It does indicate that hearing was important too, as the word 'audience' suggests. We put emphasis, rightly, on what the plays look like and how they get their ideas across visually, but perhaps we do not sufficiently recognise the importance of how the plays sound and what this means for the way we interpret them.

Printing had been introduced in England over a hundred years earlier, but not all plays of Shakespeare's time were printed. There was no money for playwrights in the printed word. Shakespeare made his living as part-owner of a theatre. There were audiences of around 2,000 in some theatres and some people could not read. To be illiterate was not a sign of a lack of education. The ability to listen and remember was vital. Blank verse helped actors to memorise long speeches. Some of the actors also might not have been able to read, and all of them would have had to memorise different parts regularly. They acted every afternoon, except Sundays and during Lent, and put on a different play each day, repeating some later on. A leading actor could have had to remember about 4,800 lines a week.

We find many variations in the spelling of words. Printing was gradually standardising spelling, but in the records of Shakespeare's time, we can see many variants on the same words. For example the name Hamlet, which he made so famous, took several forms. Shakespeare had a friend in Stratford called Hamnet/Hamlet/Hamblet. The writer's own name was written in various records as Shakspere, Shaxpere, Shagspere, Shakespeare, Shackspeare and Willielmo Shackespere among others. Listeners are able to hear double meanings in words and to enjoy the rich complexity of meaning, whereas spelling and reading can restrict our full appreciation of subtlety. Perhaps Shakespeare intended a joke in the play title *The Comedy of Errors/Eros* (Eros is the Greek god of love).

There are many jokes in Shakespeare's plays which rely on listening, but there are also many serious words, in his tragedies and histories as well as his comedies, which gain an added richness from double meaning. In *Macbeth* there are some double meanings which are more noticeable if they are listened to, as opposed to being read on the page. The word 'rapt' is used about Macbeth several times. It means that he is seized in a trance and is connected with the words 'rapture' and 'raped'. However, if an audience 'hears' the play, another sound meaning emerges. 'Wrapped' adds another dimension: the sense of everyone being cloaked and secretive comes across, as well as the image of Macbeth trying on the clothes of a king. The witches, and other people in the play, use the greeting 'All hail.' This spelling is the same as the word for 'hailstorm', but the meaning is so widely different that it is easy to miss the irony that the witches greet people with storms.

The play is very concerned with hearing different meanings (or double meaings) in what is said. The witches

> 'palter with us in a double sense'

as Macbeth discovers to his cost. He interprets

> 'No man of woman born shall harm Macbeth'

to mean that no man at all will harm him. However, he also uses double meaning himself. He has allowed his wife, whom he dearly loves, to persuade him to murder Duncan. When Duncan's body is discovered, he says to the assembled thanes,

> 'Th'expedition of my violent love / Outrun the pauser, reason'

He knows they will interpret

> 'my violent love'

as the passion of his love for Duncan. A listener can interpret it as his love for his wife. It is very difficult, and could be distorting to the action of the play, to bring out these meanings visually. They rely on sound for their full effect.

Words also echo through the play, often as an aural reminder of the presence of the witches, who are not in sight for much of the action: for example,

> **'fair, foul, double, night, blood'**

The words are spoken by various characters and have an almost subliminal effect of sending a chill down the spine at unexpected times.

Shakespeare varies the rhythm in *Macbeth* creating differences in mood and feeling. A four-beat rhythm (tetrameter) is regularly used for the witches' chants and talk with each other. This can be highlighted in performance by letting it set the pattern for their movement. Macbeth's first words in the play are in a five-beat line (pentameter).

> **'So foul and fair a day I have not seen'**

and the witches switch to this rhythm when they speak their prophecies to him:

> **'All hail Macbeth that shalt be king hereafter.'**

With this they enter his world. Rhyme is also used, often at the end of a scene, or to show a change in a scene. This can have the effect of sounding final or decided. Shakespeare's plays were not usually divided by him into acts and scenes; these have been added by printers or editors. Rhyming couplets (pairs of lines) act as oral cues, for the audience and actors, to the end of the section.

The play resembles an opera through the nature of the dialogue in the scenes between Macbeth and Lady Macbeth. They are almost duets; this is particularly striking in Act 2 Scene 2 when Macbeth has just murdered Duncan.

> **'Macbeth: This is a sorry sight.**
> **Lady Macbeth: A foolish thought to say a sorry sight.'**

This scene is full of listening, beginning with Lady Macbeth's 'Hark. Peace.', then 'the owl that shrieked' and including the voices that Macbeth has heard.

Just before Macbeth's death, he says,

> **'And be these juggling fiends no more believed**
> **That palter with us in a double sense,**
> **That keep the word of promise to our ear,**
> **And break it to our hope.'**

Shakespeare's plays are full of double sense. Are playwrights juggling fiends?

The characters

DUNCAN, King of Scotland

MALCOLM
DONALBAIN } his sons

MACBETH
BANQUO } commanders of the Scottish army

MACDUFF
LENNOX
ROSS
MENTEITH } Scottish noblemen
ANGUS
CAITHNESS

FLEANCE, Banquo's son

LADY MACBETH
LADY MACDUFF
BOY, Macduff's son
SIWARD, Earl of Northumberland, and commander of the English army
YOUNG SIWARD, his son

A CAPTAIN
A PORTER
AN OLD MAN
AN ENGLISH DOCTOR
A SCOTTISH DOCTOR
A GENTLEWOMAN, attending on Lady Macbeth
SEYTON, an Officer attending on Macbeth
Three WITCHES
HECATE
THE GHOST OF BANQUO, and other apparitions

Lords, Gentlemen, Officers, Soldiers, Murderers, Attendants, and Messengers

Macbeth

1:1

Three witches, together on a heath, call up their familiars and plan to meet with Macbeth.

1   *three* a significant number in magic and religion

3   *hurlyburly* confusion, especially political or between good and evil

4   *lost and won* the first antithesis

9   *Paddock* a common Scottish word for a frog or toad, another familiar

1–12   The witches speak with spell-like rhythm using lines with four stresses.

*How could you get an atmosphere of **filthy air** in a stage production? How would you like Graymalkin and Paddock to sound when they call?*

1:2

King Duncan and his sons receive news of the battle. Scotland is defending itself against Norwegian invaders, who have been helped by Scottish rebels and Irish mercenaries. Two accounts are received by the king.

2   *plight* the wounded state he is in

4–5   Malcolm had nearly been taken prisoner but this Sergeant rescued him.

6   *broil* disturbance

8   *spent* exhausted

12   from islands off the West coast of Scotland

13   *kernes* poor footsoldiers. *gallowglasses* horsemen with axes

14   Fortune is described as a whore, favouring the rebel with good luck.

17   *Disdaining* scorning

19   *Valour* is personified. Macbeth is like his *minion* lover or favourite

20   This is a short line. Could it be to show that the Captain is out of breath?

22   *nave* navel. *chops* jaws

Like Valour's minion, carved out his passage,
Till he faced the slave.

1:1   *Thunder and lightning. Enter three* WITCHES

FIRST WITCH   When shall we three meet again?
        In thunder, lightning, or in rain?

SECOND WITCH When the hurlyburly's done,
        When the battle's lost and won.

THIRD WITCH   That will be ere the set of sun.   5

FIRST WITCH   Where the place?

SECOND WITCH   Upon the heath.

THIRD WITCH   There to meet with Macbeth.

FIRST WITCH   I come, Graymalkin.

SECOND WITCH Paddock calls.

THIRD WITCH   Anon!   10

ALL   Fair is foul, foul is fair:
        Hover through the fog and filthy air.   [*Exeunt*

1:2   *Alarum within. Enter* DUNCAN, MALCOLM, DONALBAIN, LENNOX,
                 with ATTENDANTS, *meeting a bleeding* CAPTAIN

DUNCAN   What bloody man is that? He can report,
        As seemeth by his plight, of the revolt
        The newest state.

MALCOLM   This is the sergeant
        Who like a good and hardy soldier fought
        'Gainst my captivity. Hail, brave friend!   5
        Say to the King the knowledge of the broil
        As thou didst leave it.

CAPTAIN   Doubtful it stood,
        As two spent swimmers that do cling together
        And choke their art. The merciless Macdonwald –
        Worthy to be a rebel, for to that   10
        The multiplying villainies of nature
        Do swarm upon him – from the Western Isles
        Of kerns and gallowglasses is supplied,
        And Fortune on his damnéd quarrel smiling
        Showed like a rebel's whore. But all's too weak;   15
        For brave Macbeth – well he deserves that name –
        Disdaining Fortune, with his brandished steel,
        Which smoked with bloody execution,
        Like Valour's minion, carved out his passage,
        Till he faced the slave;   20
        Which ne'er shook hands, nor bade farewell to him,
        Till he unseamed him from the nave to th' chops,
        And fixed his head upon our battlements.

25   *whence* from where. *'gins* begins

25–8   There was also a storm as the witches appeared. Antithesis: comfort/discomfort

27–8   *spring* source: ie in the East where the sun rises but also where the Norwegians come from

30   *trust their heels* run away

31   *surveying vantage* seeing his opportunity

36   *sooth* truth

37   *cannons* there were no cannons in the 11th century

39   *Except* as if

40   *memorise another Golgotha* remind us of a graveyard. Golgotha was the name of the place where Christ was crucified.

> How could Malcolm show his recognition of the Sergeant/Captain
> (the words are used indiscriminately)? There are short lines in the
> Captain's speech (lines 20 and 41). What actions could fill the gaps?

49–50   The banners strike cold fear into the Scots.

51   *Norway himself* the king of Norway (Sweno, line 60)

54   Bellona is the goddess of war. Macbeth is her bridegroom. *lapp'd in proof* clothed in tested armour

55   *Confronted … comparisons* faced him with equal courage and skill

56   *Point* sword

DUNCAN   O valiant cousin, worthy gentleman!

CAPTAIN   As whence the sun 'gins his reflection   25
        Shipwrecking storms and direful thunders break,
        So from that spring whence comfort seemed to come
        Discomfort swells. Mark, King of Scotland, mark:
        No sooner Justice had, with Valour armed,
        Compelled these skipping kerns to trust their heels,   30
        But the Norweyan Lord, surveying vantage,
        With furbished arms and new supplies of men,
        Began a fresh assault.

DUNCAN   Dismayed not this
        Our captains, Macbeth and Banquo?

CAPTAIN   Yes –
        As sparrows eagles, or the hare the lion.   35
        If I say sooth I must report they were
        As cannons overcharged with double cracks;
        So they doubly redoubled strokes upon the foe.
        Except they meant to bathe in reeking wounds,
        Or memorise another Golgotha,   40
        I cannot tell –
        But I am faint, my gashes cry for help.

DUNCAN   So well thy words become thee as thy wounds,
        They smack of honour both. Go get him surgeons.

                                   [Exit CAPTAIN, *attended*

Enter ROSS *and* ANGUS

        Who comes here?

MALCOLM   The worthy Thane of Ross.   45

LENNOX   What a haste looks through his eyes! So should he look
        That seems to speak things strange.

ROSS   God save the King!

DUNCAN   Whence camest thou, worthy Thane?

ROSS   From Fife, great King,
        Where the Norweyan banners flout the sky,
        And fan our people cold.   50
        Norway himself, with terrible numbers,
        Assisted by that most disloyal traitor,
        The Thane of Cawdor, began a dismal conflict,
        Till that Bellona's bridegroom, lapped in proof,
        Confronted him with self-comparisons,   55
        Point against point, rebellious arm 'gainst arm,
        Curbing his lavish spirit; and, to conclude,
        The victory fell on us.

60	*craves composition* begs for a settlement
62	*disbursed* paid out. *Saint Colme's Inch* Inchcomb, an island in the Firth of Forth
63	*dollars* silver coins
66	*former title* the last name given to the Thane of Cawdor was 'most disloyal traitor' (line 52)
68	*lost … won* antithesis
65–8	rhyming lines. What effect does this have?

Macbeth's heroic character is established here. Later in the play, people use very different descriptions of him (for example, Act 4 Scene 3, line 12 **tyrant**).

The king was told that the battle had swung from the Norwegians winning to the Scots being on top and back again. Macbeth and Banquo were the heroes of the day and Macbeth in the end brought about victory for Scotland.

1:3

The witches prepare a spell to bewitch Macbeth. They prophesy great futures for Macbeth and Banquo. Macbeth is very affected. Ross arrives with a message for Macbeth from King Duncan. It is strangely coincidental.

2	Witches were thought by some to make pigs and other animals fall ill.
6	*Aroint* go away. *rump fed* well fed on rump steaks; or fat bottomed. *ronyon* a term of abuse/French word for kidney
7	*Tiger* a ship that had arrived in London in 1606 after 567 storm-tossed days
8–11 and 18	In various stories told by different groups of people, the following attributes were given to witches: that they could float in sieves (the Berwick witches claimed this in their trial), take the shape of any animal they chose, sell winds wrapped in a napkin, and drain the body fluids needed for life.
17	*card* either a compass or a sailors' map
21	*forbid* cursed
22 and 35	Notice the number, three × three.
23	He shall waste away.

16

DUNCAN	Great happiness!	
ROSS	That now	
	Sweno, the Norways' King, craves composition.	60
	Nor would we deign him burial of his men	
	Till he disburséd, at Saint Colme's Inch,	
	Ten thousand dollars to our general use.	
DUNCAN	No more that Thane of Cawdor shall deceive	
	Our bosom interest. Go pronounce his present death,	65
	And with his former title greet Macbeth.	
ROSS	I'll see it done.	
DUNCAN	What he hath lost, noble Macbeth hath won.	

[*Exeunt*

1:3   *Thunder. Enter the three* WITCHES

FIRST WITCH   Where has thou been, sister?

SECOND WITCH Killing swine.

THIRD WITCH   Sister, where thou?

FIRST WITCH   A sailor's wife had chestnuts in her lap,
And munched, and munched, and munched – 'Give me,' quoth I.   5
'Aroint thee, witch!' the rump-fed ronyon cries.
Her husband's to Aleppo gone, master o' the *Tiger*;
     But in a sieve I'll thither sail,
     And like a rat without a tail,
I'll do, I'll do, and I'll do.   10

SECOND WITCH I'll give thee a wind.

FIRST WITCH   Th'art kind.

THIRD WITCH   And I another.

FIRST WITCH   I myself have all the other;
And the very ports they blow,   15
All the quarters that they know
I' the shipman's card.
I'll drain him dry as hay;
Sleep shall neither night nor day
Hang upon his penthouse lid;   20
He shall live a man forbid.
Weary sev'n-nights nine times nine
Shall he dwindle, peak, and pine.

24   *bark* ship

33   *posters* speedy travellers

35–6   This describes a to-and-fro dance of three steps forward and three back.

> Do the witches have anything with them, to hold the winds perhaps? What does the first witch do with the thumb? Do they circle round Macbeth when they hail him? Do they touch him?

38   Antithesis. What is *foul* and what is *fair* about this day for Macbeth?

42–3   *aught … question* spirits do not wish to be questioned (compare Act 4 Scene 1, line 75)

48   *All hail* Greetings

53   *fantastical* imaginary (compare line 139 *whose murder yet is but fantastical*)

57   *rapt* in a trance (a modern audience could also hear 'wrapped')

58–9   *seeds … grain* This imagery is appropriate for Banquo.

Though his bark cannot be lost,
Yet it shall be tempest-tossed. 25
Look what I have.

SECOND WITCH Show me, show me.

FIRST WITCH Here I have a pilot's thumb,
Wrecked as homeward he did come. [*Drum within*

THIRD WITCH A drum, a drum! 30
Macbeth doth come.

ALL The Weird Sisters, hand in hand,
Posters of the sea and land,
Thus do go about, about,
Thrice to thine, and thrice to mine, 35
And thrice again, to make up nine.
Peace! – the charm's wound up.

Enter **MACBETH** *and* **BANQUO**

MACBETH So foul and fair a day I have not seen.

BANQUO How far is't called to Forres? What are these,
So withered, and so wild in their attire, 40
That look not like th' inhabitants o' th' earth,
And yet are on't? Live you? Or are you aught
That man may question? You seem to understand me,
By each at once her choppy finger laying
Upon her skinny lips. You should be women, 45
And yet your beards forbid me to interpret
That you are so.

MACBETH Speak, if you can; what are you?

FIRST WITCH All hail, Macbeth! Hail to thee, Thane of Glamis!

SECOND WITCH All hail, Macbeth! Hail to thee, Thane of Cawdor!

THIRD WITCH All hail, Macbeth, that shalt be King hereafter! 50

BANQUO Good sir, why do you start, and seem to fear
Things that do sound so fair? I' th' name of truth,
Are ye fantastical, or that indeed
Which outwardly ye show? My noble partner
You greet with present grace, and great prediction 55
Of noble having and of royal hope,
That he seems rapt withal. To me you speak not,
If you can look into the seeds of time,
And say which grain will grow, and which will not,
Speak then to me, who neither beg nor fear 60
Your favours nor your hate.

FIRST WITCH Hail!

SECOND WITCH Hail!

67	*get*	beget, be the father of
70	*imperfect*	they have not told enough
71	*Sinel*	Macbeth's father

75–6 Does Macbeth know about Cawdor's treason (lines 53–8)? It is already known by the king (Act 1 Scene 2, line 65). Is this a mistake or does it just add to the misty confusion of battle and weather (lines 110–14)? Or is Macbeth playing with deceit?

76	*intelligence*	knowledge

78 *S.D.* An early stage would have had a trapdoor.

81	*corporal*	having a body

82 Breath on a cold day is misty.

84	*insane root*	a plant which produces visions

> Macbeth and Banquo are coming back from battle. How could you show that they are tired, possibly wounded, but also high from their success?

92–3 Duncan is so amazed at and full of praise for Macbeth's achievements that he cannot speak.

96	*Nothing afeared of*	not at all afraid of
98	*post*	messenger

THIRD WITCH   Hail!

FIRST WITCH   Lesser than Macbeth, and greater.   **65**

SECOND WITCH Not so happy, yet much happier.

THIRD WITCH   Thou shalt get kings, though thou be none.
So all hail, Macbeth and Banquo.

FIRST WITCH   Banquo and Macbeth, all hail!

MACBETH   Stay, you imperfect speakers, tell me more.   **70**
By Sinel's death I know I am Thane of Glamis,
But how of Cawdor? The Thane of Cawdor lives,
A prosperous gentleman; and to be king
Stands not within the prospect of belief,
No more than to be Cawdor. Say from whence   **75**
You owe this strange intelligence, or why
Upon this blasted heath you stop our way
With such prophetic greeting. Speak, I charge you.

                                      [**WITCHES** *vanish*

BANQUO   The earth hath bubbles, as the water has,
And these are of them. Whither are they vanished?   **80**

MACBETH   Into the air; and what seemed corporal melted
As breath into the wind. Would they had stayed!

BANQUO   Were such things here as we do speak about,
Or have we eaten on the insane root
That takes the reason prisoner?   **85**

MACBETH   Your children shall be kings.

BANQUO   You shall be king.

MACBETH   And Thane of Cawdor too; went it not so?

BANQUO   To the selfsame tune and words. Who's here?

Enter **ROSS** *and* **ANGUS**

ROSS   The King hath happily received, Macbeth,
The news of thy success; and when he reads   **90**
Thy personal venture in the rebels' fight,
His wonders and his praises do contend
Which should be thine or his. Silenced with that,
In viewing o'er the rest o' th' selfsame day,
He finds thee in the stout Norweyan ranks,   **95**
Nothing afeard of what thyself didst make,
Strange images of death. As thick as hail
Came post with post, and every one did bear
Thy praises in his kingdom's great defence,
And poured them down before him.

ANGUS   We are sent   **100**
To give thee from our royal master thanks;
Only to herald thee into his sight,

104	*earnest* small first payment as a promise of more
108–9	clothing image
112	*line* strengthen, like the lining of a coat – clothing image
113	*vantage* aid
114	*in his country's wrack* for the destruction of his country
115	*capital* punishable by death
115–16	A prediction about Macbeth also.
120	*trusted home* if it is completely to be trusted
121	*enkindle you unto* spark off your motivation for
125	*betray 's* betray us
126	Banquo speaks to Ross and Angus alone. Why? Is this simply a playwright's device to leave Macbeth alone or is he telling them something?

When Ross and Angus enter, two very different worlds are seen close together: the witches and the king's official messengers. Would it be appropriate to use different levels on a stage to indicate this? What lighting or sound could help to achieve this sense of difference? Or would you make the difference in the acting, tones of voice, manner?

127	The *two truths* are the two titles which he has been given: one he knew about already; one is explained by Ross and Angus.
128	*swelling act* developing play
129	*imperial theme* becoming king
130	*soliciting* dealing (has this a hint of prostitution for modern ears?)
135	*horrid image* of himself murdering Duncan
136	*knock* remember this word later in the play
137	*Against the use of nature* unnaturally
137–8	Real things we fear are not as frightening as fears we imagine.
139	*fantastical* imaginary
140	*single state of man* a man is one entity with body and soul
140–1	I cannot act because the things I imagine are so overwhelming.
141–2	Antithesis.

Not pay thee.

ROSS And, for an earnest of a greater honour,
He bade me, from him, call thee Thane of Cawdor; **105**
In which addition, hail, most worthy Thane,
For it is thine.

BANQUO [*Aside*] What, can the devil speak true?

MACBETH The Thane of Cawdor lives. Why do you dress me
In borrowed robes?

ANGUS Who was the Thane lives yet,
But under heavy judgement bears that life **110**
Which he deserves to lose. Whether he was combined
With those of Norway, or did line the rebel
With hidden help and vantage, or that with both
He laboured in his country's wrack, I know not;
But treasons capital, confessed and proved, **115**
Have overthrown him.

MACBETH [*Aside*] Glamis, and Thane of Cawdor;
The greatest is behind. [*To* ROSS *and* ANGUS]
Thanks for your pains.
[*Aside to* BANQUO] Do you not hope your children shall be kings,
When those that gave the Thane of Cawdor to me
Promised no less to them?

BANQUO [*Aside to* MACBETH] That , trusted home, **120**
Might yet enkindle you unto the crown,
Besides the Thane of Cawdor. But 'tis strange;
And oftentimes to win us to our harm,
The instruments of darkness tell us truths,
Win us with honest trifles, to betray 's **125**
In deepest consequence.
[*To* ROSS *and* ANGUS] Cousins, a word I pray you.

MACBETH [*Aside*] Two truths are told
As happy prologues to the swelling act
Of the imperial theme. [*Aloud*] I thank you, gentlemen.
[*Aside*] This supernatural soliciting **130**
Cannot be ill, cannot be good. If ill,
Why hath it given me earnest of success,
Commencing in a truth? I am Thane of Cawdor.
If good, why do I yield to that suggestion
Whose horrid image doth unfix my hair, **135**
And make my seated heart knock at my ribs,
Against the use of nature? Present fears
Are less than horrible imaginings:
My thought, whose murder yet is but fantastical,
Shakes so my single state of man that function **140**
Is smothered in surmise, and nothing is

23

Macbeth

Look how our partner's rapt.

Where could Macbeth go for his asides? In your staging would you leave the witches in view for the audience although not seen by the characters? How could you show Macbeth drawn into their influence?

Macbeth is **rapt**. Watch out for other times when he is in a world of his own horrible imaginings. He sees a dagger and a ghost at different times later in the play.

The witches told Macbeth that he would become first Thane of Cawdor and then king. They told Banquo he would father kings. Ross arrived to tell Macbeth the king was promoting him to Thane of Cawdor. Macbeth, amazed by the witches' truth, fantasised about becoming king.

1:4

The scene begins peacefully, showing order in the kingdom soon to be disrupted. Duncan thanks Macbeth and Banquo, then makes his own son, Malcolm, heir to the Scottish throne. The party sets off to feast and spend the night at Macbeth's castle.

But what is not.

BANQUO   Look how our partner's rapt.

MACBETH [*Aside*] If chance will have me king, why, chance may crown me,
    Without my stir.

BANQUO   New honours come upon him,
    Like our strange garments, cleave not to their mould   145
    But with the aid of use.

MACBETH [*Aside*]   Come what come may,
    Time and the hour runs through the roughest day.

BANQUO   Worthy Macbeth, we stay upon your leisure.

MACBETH   Give me your favour; my dull brain was wrought
    With things forgotten. Kind gentlemen, your pains   150
    Are registered where every day I turn
    The leaf to read them. Let us toward the King.
    [*Aside to* BANQUO] Think upon what hath chanced; and at more time,
    The interim having weighed it, let us speak
    Our free hearts each to each other.   155

BANQUO   Very gladly.

MACBETH   Till then, enough. – Come friends.   [*Exeunt*

`1:4`   *Flourish. Enter* DUNCAN, MALCOLM, DONALBAIN,
                    LENNOX, *and* ATTENDANTS

DUNCAN   Is execution done on Cawdor? Are not
    Those in commission yet returned?

MALCOLM   My liege,
    They are not yet come back; but I have spoke
    With one that saw him die, who did report
    That very frankly he confessed his treasons,   5
    Implored your Highness' pardon, and set forth
    A deep repentance. Nothing in his life
    Became him like the leaving it; he died
    As one that had been studied in his death,
    To throw away the dearest thing he owed   10

25

11–12 We cannot tell a man's character from his face.

14 This line is broken by the arrival of Macbeth.

18–20 I wish you had deserved fewer thanks and then I might have been able to thank you enough. Duncan could be hiding a fear that Macbeth expects to be king after Duncan's death.

20–1 A rhyming couplet. What effect could Duncan want here?

22–7 Does Macbeth overstate his loyalty?

28 Banquo again is associated with natural growth.

34 *Wanton* unrestrained

> *The grouping is important in this scene because it is partly about the different status of individuals in society now that the war is over. In what order do Macbeth and Banquo enter? How does Duncan greet them? Would it be in the same way?*

37 *establish our estate* name as the next king

39 *Prince of Cumberland* like today's Prince of Wales, next in line to the throne

40 We do not only honour him with this, but all of you who have deserved it; or: The title is only for Malcolm and no one else. Is it clear what Duncan means by this?

42 *Inverness* Macbeth's castle

44 Any rest which is not used to serve you seems like hard work.

45 *harbinger* messenger

47 *Cawdor* Duncan reminds Macbeth of his recent gift to him of Cawdor

As 'twere a careless trifle.

DUNCAN   There's no art
To find the mind's construction in the face:
He was a gentleman on whom I built
An absolute trust.

Enter MACBETH, BANQUO, ROSS *and* ANGUS

                              O worthiest cousin!
The sin of my ingratitude even now   **15**
Was heavy on me. Thou art so far before
That swiftest wing of recompense is slow
To overtake thee. Would thou hadst less deserved,
That the proportion both of thanks and payment
Might have been mine. Only I have left to say,   **20**
More is thy due than more than all can pay.

MACBETH   The service and the loyalty I owe,
In doing it, pays itself. Your Highness' part
Is to receive our duties; and our duties
Are to your throne and state, children and servants,   **25**
Which do but what they should by doing every thing
Safe toward your love and honour.

DUNCAN   Welcome hither.
I have begun to plant thee, and will labour
To make thee full of growing. – Noble Banquo,
That hast no less deserved, nor must be known   **30**
No less to have done so, let me infold thee,
And hold thee to my heart.

BANQUO   There if I grow,
The harvest is your own.

DUNCAN   My plenteous joys,
Wanton in fulness, seek to hide themselves
In drops of sorrow. – Sons, kinsmen, thanes,   **35**
And you whose places are the nearest, know,
We will establish our estate upon
Our eldest, Malcolm, whom we name hereafter
The Prince of Cumberland; which honour must
Not unaccompanied invest him only,   **40**
But signs of nobleness, like stars, shall shine
On all deservers. [*To* MACBETH] From hence to Inverness,
And bind us further to you.

MACBETH   The rest is labour, which is not used for you.
I'll be myself the harbinger, and make joyful   **45**
The hearing of my wife with your approach;
So humbly take my leave.

DUNCAN   My worthy Cawdor!

52 *wink at* seem not to see

52–3 Let that happen which eyes will not want to look upon.

54 *he* Macbeth

55 *in his commendations* in praising him

56 The meal as a sign of trust and togetherness is important.

58 *peerless* unequalled. *kinsman* Macbeth was Duncan's first cousin

> *Where and how does Malcolm stand and what happens when Duncan makes him Prince of Cumberland? How do the other thanes and attendants react? Do they approve? Do they look at Macbeth and Banquo wondering how they take it?*

This scene is full of falsely polite or diplomatic language. There is more from Lady Macbeth and Duncan when he arrives at the castle in Scene 6.

Duncan greeted Macbeth and Banquo with compliments and thanks for their heroism. He made Malcolm Prince of Cumberland, which Macbeth regarded, privately, as an obstacle to himself becoming king.

1:5

Lady Macbeth enters for the first time, reading a letter from her husband that tells of the witches' prophecy and of his recent promotion. A messenger informs her that Duncan is coming to stay at her home. She prepares herself, and then Macbeth, for the ambitious, evil act to come.

1 *They* the witches

2 *the perfectest report* Has Macbeth made enquiries about the witches?

5 *rapt* the third time this word is used of him

6 *missives* messengers

6–7 *all-hailed* greeted

8–9 *referred me to the coming on of time* told me about the future

13 Macbeth has not mentioned what the witches prophesied for Banquo. Why?

16 *milk of human kindness* the gentleness of human nature (learned at a mother's breast). Remember witches dry up body fluids.

17 *wouldst* would like to

19 *illness should attend it* evil that should go with it. *What thou wouldst highly* what you want, which is high up

20 *That wouldst thou holily:* you want to get in an honourable way

MACBETH [*Aside*] The Prince of Cumberland! That is a step
    On which I must fall down, or else o'erleap,
    For in my way it lies. Stars, hide your fires,   **50**
    Let not light see my black and deep desires;
    The eye wink at the hand; yet let that be
    Which the eye fears, when it is done, to see.

                                            [*Exit*

DUNCAN   True, worthy Banquo; he is full so valiant,
    And in his commendations I am fed: **55**
    It is a banquet to me. Let's after him,
    Whose care is gone before to bid us welcome.
    It is a peerless kinsman.

                                   [*Flourish. Exeunt*

1:5   *Enter* LADY MACBETH, *reading a letter*

LADY MACBETH *They met me in the day of success; and I*
have learned by the perfectest report they have more in
them than mortal knowledge. When I burned in desire
to question them further, they made themselves air,
into which they vanished. Whiles I stood rapt in the   **5**
wonder of it, came missives from the King, who all-
hailed me "Thane of Cawdor", by which title before
these Weird Sisters saluted me, and referred me to the
coming on of time with "Hail, King that shalt be!"
This have I thought good to deliver thee, my dearest   **10**
partner of greatness, that thou mightst not lose the
dues of rejoicing by being ignorant of what greatness
is promised thee. Lay it to thy heart, and farewell.

    Glamis thou art, and Cawdor; and shalt be
    What thou art promised. Yet do I fear thy nature;   **15**
    It is too full o' th' milk of human kindness
    To catch the nearest way. Thou wouldst be great,
    Art not without ambition, but without
    The illness should attend it. What thou wouldst highly,
    That wouldst thou holily; wouldst not play false,   **20**

21–2 *Thou'dst have … if thou have it* you want to have the crown but you have to do something first if you are to get it. The very complicated lines here show her struggling with problems. What problems are they?

23–4 You fear to do it (the murder) but you want to do it also.

24 *Hie* hurry

26 *chastise* whip

27 *golden round* crown

28 *metaphysical* supernatural

32 *Would have informed* your master would have given us notice for preparing for the king's arrival

34 *had the speed of* went faster than

35 *for breath* for lack of breath

36 *Give him tending* look after him

> What does Lady Macbeth do with the letter? Do you think this is the first time she has read it or has she been dwelling on it for some time? Does she **lay it to her heart** or burn it or lock it away? Would you emphasise **shalt be** with an action? How does she react to the news that the king is coming?

37–8 Refers to the superstition that ravens tell of horrors to come.

38 *fatal* either Duncan is going to die or his fate is waiting for him

40 *mortal* deadly/human. *unsex* Shakespeare made up this word

42 *direst* bitterest

42–3 *Make thick … remorse* pity cannot flow along the veins and reach the heart

43 *remorse* pity

44–6 So that no natural feeling of pity may disturb my terrible purpose and stop me from achieving my end.

44 *compunctious* prickings of compassion

45 *fell* fierce

47 *gall* a bitter-tasting secretion of the liver. Female saints, on the other hand, were said to secrete milk, not blood, when tortured. *ministers* spirits

48 *sightless* invisible

49 *wait on nature's mischief* serve evil in nature

50 *pall* sheet up like a dead body. *dunnest* darkest

51 *my keen knife* Does she mean to stab Duncan herself?

52 *blanket* suggests the world is sleeping

56–7 The present time does not know what is to come but I do. I see it now.

And yet wouldst wrongly win. Thou'dst have, great Glamis,
That which cries 'Thus thou must do' if thou have it;
And that which rather thou dost fear to do
Than wishest should be undone. Hie thee thither,
That I may pour my spirits in thine ear,   **25**
And chastise with the valour of my tongue
All that impedes thee from the golden round,
Which fate and metaphysical aid doth seem
To have thee crowned withal.

Enter a MESSENGER

What is your tidings?

MESSENGER   The King comes here tonight.

LADY MACBETH   Thou'rt mad to say it.   **30**
Is not thy master with him – who, were't so,
Would have informed for preparation?

MESSENGER   So please you, it is true; our Thane is coming.
One of my fellows had the speed of him,
Who, almost dead for breath, had scarcely more   **35**
Than would make up his message.

LADY MACBETH   Give him tending;
He brings great news.

[Exit MESSENGER

The raven himself is hoarse
That croaks the fatal entrance of Duncan
Under my battlements. Come, you spirits
That tend on mortal thoughts, unsex me here,   **40**
And fill me, from the crown to the toe, top-full
Of direst cruelty. Make thick my blood,
Stop up th' access and passage to remorse,
That no compunctious visitings of nature
Shake my fell purpose, nor keep peace between   **45**
The effect and it. Come to my woman's breasts,
And take my milk for gall, you murd'ring ministers,
Wherever in your sightless substances
You wait on nature's mischief. Come, thick night,
And pall thee in the dunnest smoke of hell,   **50**
That my keen knife see not the wound it makes,
Nor heaven peep through the blanket of the dark,
To cry 'Hold, hold!'

Enter MACBETH

Great Glamis! Worthy Cawdor!
Greater than both, by the all-hail hereafter!
Thy letters have transported me beyond   **55**
This ignorant present, and I feel now
The future in the instant.

31

58 *Duncan* Macbeth does not say 'the King'. Why?

62–3 *To beguile the time / Look like the time* to deceive people here and now, do what is expected of you here and now

65 *serpent* the devil is a serpent in the Bible. He tempts Eve to eat from the forbidden tree.

67 *into my dispatch* into my hands to do it

71 A change of expression leads people to suspect.

72 Does she do all the rest? Does he leave it to her to do later?

Lady Macbeth prays directly to spirits of evil. How could you show this as a reversal of prayer to the spirits of good? She has just asked to have her sexuality changed so how does she welcome her husband? Does she see him as soon as he comes in? What action could accompany **Your face** and **Only look up**?

Lady Macbeth echoes the words used by the witches, **shalt be** and **all-hail** (Act 1, Scene 3, lines 48–50) and also Macbeth's letter in this scene (lines 7 and 10).

Lady Macbeth read her husband's letter and determined that Macbeth should become king. She asked evil spirits to give her strength and when Macbeth entered she was forceful with him to overcome his weakening ambition.

1:6

The king, his sons and thanes arrive at Macbeth's castle and are welcomed by Lady Macbeth.

S.D. *Hautboys* oboes. *Torches* Is it evening time?

1 *seat* position

4 *martlet* house-martin, a bird that was supposed to build its nest in the roofs of peaceful or holy buildings. *approve* prove

5 *mansionry* nest-building place

6 *jutty* overhanging part

7 *coign of vantage* suitable corner

8 *pendent* hanging. *procreant* for laying eggs in

11–14 Sometimes we cause trouble because we are loved. We thank you for the trouble you are taking and ask God to reward you.

MACBETH   My dearest love,
        Duncan comes here tonight.

LADY MACBETH   And when goes hence?

MACBETH   Tomorrow, as he purposes.

LADY MACBETH   O, never
        Shall sun that morrow see!   **60**
        Your face, my Thane, is a book where men
        May read strange matters. To beguile the time,
        Look like the time; bear welcome in your eye,
        Your hand, your tongue; look like the innocent flower,
        But be the serpent under't. He that's coming   **65**
        Must be provided for; and you shall put
        This night's great business into my dispatch,
        Which shall to all our nights and days to come
        Give solely sovereign sway and masterdom.

MACBETH   We will speak further.

LADY MACBETH   Only look up clear;   **70**
        To alter favour ever is to fear.
        Leave all the rest to me.   [*Exeunt*

1:6   *Hautboys and torches. Enter* DUNCAN, MALCOLM, DONALBAIN,
              BANQUO, LENNOX, MACDUFF, ROSS, ANGUS, *and* ATTENDANTS

DUNCAN   This castle hath a pleasant seat; the air
        Nimbly and sweetly recommends itself
        Unto our gentle senses.

BANQUO   This guest of summer,
        The temple-haunting martlet, does approve
        By his loved mansionry that the heaven's breath   **5**
        Smells wooingly here: no jutty, frieze,
        Buttress, nor coign of vantage, but this bird
        Hath made his pendent bed and procreant cradle.
        Where they most breed and haunt, I have observed
        The air is delicate.

                        Enter LADY MACBETH

DUNCAN   See, see, our honoured hostess.   **10**
        The love that follows us sometime is our trouble,
        Which still we thank as love. Herein I teach you,
        How you shall bid God 'ield us for your pains,
        And thank us for your trouble.

Macbeth

All our service,
In every point twice done, and then done double.

15 *double* twice but also two-faced

17–20 Because of your honours, both in the past, and the many recently, we shall always pray for you.

21 *coursed him at the heels* chased close behind him

22 *purveyor* officer who travelled before the king to make sure of provisions

23 *holp* helped

26–8 *in compt … own* must always be accountably at your service, simply giving back to you what is yours (as Duncan owns everything, being the king)

This scene contrasts with the last as it describes healthy breeding and not milk turned to gall. How could you show this? The men have returned from battle, finally arriving at a welcoming castle and feast. How does Lady Macbeth greet them? Do they find her attractive? Macbeth is noticeably not here to welcome Duncan. Would you let an audience see him elsewhere?

Scene 5 of Act 1 uses the language of hell and Scene 6 the language of heaven.

Duncan arrived with his thanes and attendants at Macbeth's castle. Lady Macbeth welcomed him. The king noticed that Macbeth was not present.

1:7

Duncan and the guests are banqueting off stage and Macbeth has left the table to consider his plan for murder. He is joined by his wife.

S.D. *Sewer* originally meant a taster of the king's meal

1 *it* the murder

3 *trammel up* hinder as with a net or rope. *consequence* what might happen afterwards

4 *surcease* death

6 now and on this earth. *shoal* a shallow place in a sea or river, liable to cause shipwreck

7 *jump* risk or forget about. *the life to come* our afterlife

8 *judgement* punishment. *here* on earth. *that* so that

9 *Bloody instructions* how to commit murderous acts

10 *th' inventor* the person who taught them. *even-handed* fair

LADY MACBETH   All our service,
  In every point twice done, and then done double,   15
  Were poor and single business to contend
  Against those honours deep and broad wherewith
  Your Majesty loads our house. For those of old,
  And the late dignities heaped up to them,
  We rest your hermits.

DUNCAN   Where's the Thane of Cawdor?   20
  We coursed him at the heels, and had a purpose
  To be his purveyor; but he rides well,
  And his great love, sharp as his spur, hath holp him
  To his home before us. Fair and noble hostess,
  We are your guest tonight.

LADY MACBETH   *   Your servants ever   25
  Have theirs, themselves, and what is theirs, in compt,
  To make their audit at your Highness' pleasure,
  Still to return your own.

DUNCAN   Give me your hand;
  Conduct me to mine host. We love him highly,
  And shall continue our graces towards him.   30
  By your leave, hostess.   [*Exeunt*

1:7   *Hautboys and torches. Enter, and pass over the stage, a* SEWER *and*
              divers SERVANTS *with dishes and service. Then enter* MACBETH

MACBETH   If it were done, when 'tis done, then 'twere well
  It were done quickly. If the assassination
  Could trammel up the consequence, and catch,
  With his surcease, success; that but this blow
  Might be the be-all and the end-all – here,   5
  But here, upon this bank and shoal of time –
  We'd jump the life to come. But in these cases
  We still have judgement here – that we but teach
  Bloody instructions, which, being taught, return
  To plague th' inventor. This even-handed justice   10

11 *Commends* offers. *ingredience* contents. *chalice* holy communion cup or ceremonial vessel

17 *faculties* kingly powers

18 *clear* free from guilt

19 *trumpet-tongued* trumpets are expected to be the symbol for the day of the Last Judgement, when some people believe that we will be judged for our sins and virtues

20 *his taking-off* murder

21 *babe* implies both innocence and Jesus

22 *cherubin* angels

23 *sightless couriers of the air* winds

24 So that the wicked deed can be seen by all. *blow* perhaps recalls the explosion of the Gunpowder Plot

25–8 I have no motivation for this intended murder, but only ambition. The image is of a man mounting a horse too energetically and falling over the other side!

Would Macbeth have a wine glass or anything else? Would there be sounds from the meal near by? Would you want the banquet to be visible to the audience?

34 *would* should. *worn* clothing

36 *dressed* clothing

37 *green and pale* with a hangover. Could either of them be a little drunk?

39 *Such I account thy love* your love is like a drunken promise

42 *ornament of life* the crown

45 *cat i' the adage* the cat wants to eat fish but will not wet her feet

47 *none* subhuman. *beast* emphasising the contrast with *man*

48 *break this enterprise* suggest this project (murdering Duncan). Does this imply that they had discussed it previously at some time, before or after Macbeth's meeting with the witches? Note the use of euphemism.

Commends th' ingredience of our poisoned chalice
To our own lips. He's here in double trust:
First, as I am his kinsman and his subject –
Strong both against the deed; then, as his host,
Who should against his murderer shut the door,   15
Not bear the knife myself. Besides, this Duncan
Hath borne his faculties so meek, hath been
So clear in his great office, that his virtues
Will plead like angels trumpet-tongued against
The deep damnation of his taking-off;   20
And Pity, like a naked new-born babe,
Striding the blast, or heaven's cherubin, horsed
Upon the sightless couriers of the air,
Shall blow the horrid deed in every eye,
That tears shall drown the wind. I have no spur   25
To prick the sides of my intent, but only
Vaulting ambition, which o'erleaps itself
And falls on the other –

Enter Lady Macbeth

How now, what news?

Lady Macbeth He has almost supped. Why have you left the chamber?

Macbeth   Hath he asked for me?

Lady Macbeth   Know you not he has?   30

Macbeth   We will proceed no further in this business.
He hath honoured me of late, and I have bought
Golden opinions from all sorts of people,
Which would be worn now in their newest gloss,
Not cast aside so soon.

Lady Macbeth   Was the hope drunk   35
Wherein you dressed yourself? Hath it slept since?
And wakes it now to look so green and pale
At what it did so freely? From this time
Such I account thy love. Art thou afeard
To be the same in thine own act and valour   40
As thou art in desire? Wouldst thou have that
Which thou esteem'st the ornament of life,
And live a coward in thine own esteem,
Letting 'I dare not' wait upon 'I would',
Like the poor cat i' the adage?

Macbeth   Prithee, peace.   45
I dare do all that may become a man;
Who dares do more is none.

Lady Macbeth   What beast was't then
That made you break this enterprise to me?
When you durst do it, then you were a man;

52 *Did then adhere* were then appropriate

54 The historical Lady Macbeth had a child by a previous husband.

60 *But* Only. The metaphor may refer to a crossbowman tightening the bowstring.

61 *asleep* sleep relates to vulnerability and innocence

63 *chamberlains* servants for the bedroom

64 *wassail* drinking toasts. *convince* overpower

65 *warder* guardian

67 *limbeck* an instrument used in purifying liquids. Memory is important to both the Macbeths later in the play.

68 *drenchéd* drunk

71 *spongy* drunk

72 *quell* murder/kill

73 *mettle* the word 'metal' did not have a different spelling in the 16th century

74 *received* accepted as true

77 *other* otherwise

79 *settled* finally determined. *bend up* image of bowstring or athlete

80 *corporal agent* bodily part

82 Repetition of 'f' recalls 'fair is foul'.

*How does Lady Macbeth say **I have given suck**? Does she show pain at the memory, or is she attacking him with the notion, or something else? How does Macbeth say **Bring forth men children only**? Is he bitter, full of admiration, fear, or something else?*

Later in the play, a banquet for the thanes is shown to the audience.

Duncan and the thanes were feasting and Macbeth left the table to consider the implications of killing the king. Lady Macbeth joined him and persuaded him, by scoffing at his lack of manliness, to determine to kill Duncan. Act 2 continues with events of the same night.

And to be more than what you were, you would   **50**
Be so much more the man. Nor time, nor place,
Did then adhere, and yet you would make both;
They have made themselves, and that their fitness now
Does unmake you. I have given suck, and know
How tender 'tis to love the babe that milks me –   **55**
I would, while it was smiling in my face,
Have plucked my nipple from his boneless gums
And dashed the brains out, had I so sworn
As you have done to this.

MACBETH   If we should fail?

LADY MACBETH   We fail?
But screw your courage to the sticking-place,   **60**
And we'll not fail. When Duncan is asleep
(Whereto the rather shall his day's hard journey
Soundly invite him) his two chamberlains
Will I with wine and wassail so convince
That memory, the warder of the brain,   **65**
Shall be a fume, and the receipt of reason
A limbeck only. When in swinish sleep
Their drenchéd natures lie as in a death,
What cannot you and I perform upon
The unguardéd Duncan? What not put upon   **70**
His spongy officers, who shall bear the guilt
Of our great quell?

MACBETH   Bring forth men-children only!
For thy undaunted mettle should compose
Nothing but males. Will it not be received,
When we have marked with blood those sleepy two   **75**
Of his own chamber, and used their very daggers,
That they have done't?

LADY MACBETH   Who dares receive it other,
As we shall make our griefs and clamour roar
Upon his death?

MACBETH   I am settled, and bend up
Each corporal agent to this terrible feat.   **80**
Away, and mock the time with fairest show:
False face must hide what the false heart doth know.

                                                [Exeunt

2:1

It is after midnight. Banquo is awake with his son. They meet Macbeth, speak about the witches and Banquo goes to bed. Macbeth sees a visionary dagger floating in the air.

4	*husbandry* being careful with money
5	What else do you think he gives Fleance here?
6	*summons* a call to sleep
8–9	What do you think Banquo's evil thoughts are? See line 20.
14	*largess* generous presents
16	*shut up* is gone to bed
17–19	*Being unprepared … wrought* As we had no time to prepare, our hospitality is not as good as it could be. Is this ironic? Macbeth, after all, is planning to kill Duncan.
23	*would* would like to
25	*cleave to my consent* follow my advice or be of my party. He is ambiguously suggesting a bribe to Banquo.
26–7	*So … augment it.* as long as I do not lose my honour by trying to increase it
28	*bosom franchised* conscience free. *allegiance* oath of loyalty to a king

Does Banquo wish Fleance to overhear this conversation? How would you show this, either way? There is another opportunity here for a production to indicate the witches' influence. How could it be done?

2:1   *Enter* BANQUO, *and* FLEANCE, *with a torch before him*

BANQUO   How goes the night, boy?

FLEANCE   The moon is down; I have not heard the clock.

BANQUO   And she goes down at twelve.

FLEANCE   I take't, 'tis later, sir.

BANQUO   Hold, take my sword. There's husbandry in heaven;
           Their candles are all out. Take thee that too.   5
           A heavy summons lies like lead upon me,
           And yet I would not sleep. Merciful Powers,
           Restrain in me the curséd thoughts that nature
           Gives way to in repose. Give me my sword.

                 Enter MACBETH, *and a* SERVANT *with a torch*

           Who's there?   10

MACBETH   A friend.

BANQUO   What, sir, not yet at rest? The king's a-bed.
           He hath been in unusual pleasure, and
           Sent forth great largess to your offices.
           This diamond he greets your wife withal,   15
           By the name of most kind hostess, and shut up
           In measureless content.

MACBETH   Being unprepared,
           Our will became the servant to defect,
           Which else should free have wrought.

BANQUO   All's well.
           I dreamt last night of the three Weird Sisters.   20
           To you they have showed some truth.

MACBETH   I think not of them.
           Yet when we can entreat an hour to serve,
           We would spend it in some words upon that business,
           If you would grant the time.

BANQUO   At your kind'st leisure.

MACBETH   If you shall cleave to my consent, when 'tis,   25
           It shall make honour for you.

BANQUO   So I lose none
           In seeking to augment it, but still keep
           My bosom franchised and allegiance clear,
           I shall be counselled.

MACBETH   Good repose the while.

BANQUO   Thanks, sir; the like to you.   30

                                      [*Exeunt* BANQUO *and* FLEANCE

36   *fatal* deadly, or showing future fate

36–7   *sensible / To feeling* able to be touched

39   *heat-oppressed* feverish

40   *palpable* touchably real

41   This short line leaves space for him to pull out his real dagger.

42   *marshall'st* direct

44–5   *Mine … rest.* My eyes are tricking me, if my other senses are right; or: My eyes are right and the other senses are wrong.

46   *dudgeon* handle. *gouts* big drops

48–9   *informs / Thus* gives this impression

50–1   *wicked … sleep* later, Macbeth and Lady Macbeth cannot sleep. He is almost prophesying it here.

52   *Hecate* the witches' goddess. Witches perform at night. The 'half-world' (line 49) which is asleep is the good half. *offerings* rituals

53–4   *Alarumed … watch.* Murder is shown as a man who works at night, using the wolf's howl as his alarm.

54   *howl's* howl is.

55   *Tarquin* raped Lucrece. *ravishing strides* the steps that take him to his rape victim

57–8   This could mean either: the stones will be infected with the horror of this moment; or: because my footsteps will be heard, that will stop me committing the murder. He is undecided and half wishes to be stopped.

58   *prate* talk about

60–4   What effect is produced by having two rhyming couplets, divided by a single line?

What does Macbeth do before he sees the visionary dagger? Does the audience see the dagger? How does he react to it? What does the bell sound like? Could it remind us of the witches or sound like a funeral bell?

Compare the **horrid image** (Act 1 Scene 3, lines 135–7) of murder, which makes Macbeth's hair stand on end. He is troubled by visual imaginings.

Compare this scene with Act 1 Scene 3, which is the last time Macbeth and Banquo spoke directly together. Has their relationship changed?

Banquo and Fleance, checking the castle at midnight after the feast, met Macbeth. Banquo said how happy Duncan was with the evening's entertainment. He and Fleance went to bed. Macbeth saw a vision of a dagger and interpreted it as a sign that he should kill Duncan. He went towards Duncan's room with his own dagger in his hand.

MACBETH   Go bid thy mistress, when my drink is ready,
She strike upon the bell. Get thee to bed.   [*Exit* SERVANT
Is this a dagger which I see before me,
The handle toward my hand? Come, let me clutch thee.
I have thee not, and yet I see thee still.   35
Art thou not, fatal vision, sensible
To feeling as to sight? Or art thou but
A dagger of the mind, a false creation,
Proceeding from the heat-oppressed brain?
I see thee yet, in form as palpable   40
As this which I now draw.
Thou marshall'st me the way that I was going,
And such an instrument I was to use.
Mine eyes are made the fools o'th'other senses,
Or else worth all the rest. I see thee still;   45
And on thy blade and dudgeon gouts of blood,
Which was not so before. – There's no such thing:
It is the bloody business which informs
Thus to mine eyes. Now o'er the one half-world
Nature seems dead, and wicked dreams abuse   50
The curtained sleep. Witchcraft celebrates
Pale Hecate's offerings; and withered Murder,
Alarumed by his sentinel, the wolf,
Whose howl's his watch, thus with his stealthy pace,
With Tarquin's ravishing strides, towards his design   55
Moves like a ghost. Thou sure and firm-set earth,
Hear not my steps, which way they walk, for fear
Thy very stones prate of my whereabout.
And take the present horror from the time,
Which now suits with it. Whiles I threat, he lives;   60
Words to the heat of deeds too cold breath gives.   [*A bell rings*
I go, and it is done; the bell invites me.
Hear it not, Duncan, for it is a knell
That summons thee to heaven, or to hell.

[*Exit*

2:2

Lady Macbeth waits nervously for her husband to murder Duncan. He comes in with bloody hands and describes the deed. Lady Macbeth then sees a mistake he has made.

1–2	*drunk … bold* and *quenched … fire* are contrasts
3	*fatal bellman* remember the bell of the previous scene. A bellman rang to announce the deaths of condemned prisoners.
4	*stern'st good-night* the last good-night of death
5	*surfeited grooms* Duncan's guards, who have drunk too much
6	*mock … snores* make a mockery of their job of guarding Duncan and/or snore as loudly as Duncan is doing. *possets* hot drinks of milk and spices. People can be bewitched through their drinks.
10–11	*The attempt … Confounds us* we have been found out and not succeeded
13	*I had done't* Notice that she could not do it herself.
13	This is the only time she calls him husband.
14	*done* is echoed between Macbeth and Lady Macbeth
15	*crickets* the cricket, it is said, foretells death
16	*Did not … descended?* This is all one line of verse divided between them.
20	*sorry* pitiable. What is a *sorry sight*?
25	*two* these could be the guards of Duncan's sons
27	*hangman's* the hangman had to quarter the body also
28 and 31	*Amen* a prayer for blessing. If a person could not utter a prayer it was a sign that they had been bewitched.

The pace of the opening of the scene contrasts sharply with the previous one. How could you show the nervousness and relationship of guilt between Macbeth and Lady Macbeth? Macbeth is in a world of his own, almost in a trance, still hearing the voices in Duncan's bedroom.

The scene is full of sound and listening.

2:2   *Enter* **Lady Macbeth**

Lady Macbeth That which hath made them drunk hath made me bold;
What hath quenched them hath given me fire. Hark! – Peace:
It was the owl that shrieked, the fatal bellman,
Which gives the stern'st good-night. He is about it.
The doors are open; and the surfeited grooms   **5**
Do mock their charge with snores. I have drugged their possets,
That death and nature do contend about them,
Whether they live or die.

Macbeth [*Within*] Who's there? – What, ho!

Lady Macbeth Alack, I am afraid they have awaked,
And 'tis not done! The attempt and not the deed   **10**
Confounds us. Hark! – I laid their daggers ready,
He could not miss 'em. Had he not resembled
My father as he slept, I had done't.

                         Enter **Macbeth**

                              My husband!

Macbeth   I have done the deed. – Didst thou not hear a noise?

Lady Macbeth I heard the owl scream, and the crickets cry.   **15**
Did not you speak?

Macbeth   When?

Lady Macbeth   Now.

Macbeth   As I descended?

Lady Macbeth Ay.

Macbeth   Hark!
Who lies i' the second chamber?

Lady Macbeth   Donalbain.

Macbeth [*Looking at his hands*] This is a sorry sight.   **20**

Lady Macbeth A foolish thought, to say a sorry sight.

Macbeth   There's one did laugh in's sleep, and one cried 'Murder!'
They did wake each other. I stood and heard them;
But they did say their prayers, and addressed them
Again to sleep.

Lady Macbeth   There are two lodged together.   **25**

Macbeth   One cried 'God bless us!' and 'Amen' the other,
As they had seen me with these hangman's hands.
Listening their fear, I could not say 'Amen'
When they did say 'God bless us!'

Lady Macbeth Consider it not so deeply.   **30**

Macbeth   But wherefore could not I pronounce 'Amen'?
I had most need of blessing, and 'Amen'

45

34 *so, it will make us mad* Lady Macbeth is aware of this danger

35 *I heard a voice* Macbeth hears voices as well as seeing visions

37 *ravelled sleave* tangled silk or a ragged, frayed sleeve. Clothing imagery occurs in other places as well.

43 *sleep* How many times has Macbeth used this word from line 22 to here? What effect does this repetition have?

45 *unbend* weaken

Why did you bring these daggers from the place?

56–7 Notice the pun: *gild*, which means paint and *guilt*

57 *knocking* (remember Act 1 Scene 2, line 136). From the bell to the knocking is an enchanted or hypnotic time. Apart from there being someone at the door, the knocking could also mean his heart or his conscience.

59 *they pluck out mine eyes* he sees his guilt

62 *incarnadine* turn to blood-red

68–9 *Your constancy … unattended* your firmness has left you

How many daggers has Macbeth brought? Did he take his own with him? The moment Lady Macbeth suddenly sees the blood on his hands and on the daggers can be violently dramatic. How long would she take to realise what it meant? Why did she not see them before? The red hands and the water are connected with guilt and attempts to get rid of it. What would be an effective way of presenting this?

Stuck in my throat.

LADY MACBETH   These deeds must not be thought
After these ways; so, it will make us mad.

MACBETH   Methought I heard a voice cry 'Sleep no more!   35
Macbeth does murder sleep' – the innocent sleep,
Sleep that knits up the ravelled sleave of care,
The death of each day's life, sore labour's bath,
Balm of hurt minds, great nature's second course,
Chief nourisher in life's feast, –

LADY MACBETH   What do you mean?   40

MACBETH   Still it cried 'Sleep no more!' to all the house;
'Glamis hath murdered sleep, and therefore Cawdor
Shall sleep no more; Macbeth shall sleep no more'.

LADY MACBETH   Who was it that thus cried? Why, worthy Thane,
You do unbend your noble strength to think   45
So brainsickly of things. Go get some water,
And wash this filthy witness from your hand.
Why did you bring these daggers from the place?
They must lie there. Go, carry them, and smear
The sleepy grooms with blood.

MACBETH   I'll go no more: 50
I am afraid to think what I have done;
Look on't again I dare not.

LADY MACBETH   Infirm of purpose!
Give me the daggers. The sleeping and the dead
Are but as pictures; 'tis the eye of childhood
That fears a painted devil. If he do bleed,   55
I'll gild the faces of the grooms withal.
For it must seem their guilt.

                                                   [*Exit. Knocking within*

MACBETH   Whence is that knocking?
How is't with me, when every noise appals me?
What hands are here? Ha! They pluck out mine eyes.
Will all great Neptune's ocean wash this blood   60
Clean from my hand? No, this my hand will rather
The multitudinous seas incarnadine,
Making the green one red.

Enter LADY MACBETH

LADY MACBETH   My hands are of your colour; but I shame
To wear a heart so white. [*Knocking*] I hear a knocking   65
At the south entry. Retire we to our chamber.
A little water clears us of this deed;
How easy is it then! Your constancy
Hath left you unattended. [*Knocking*] Hark, more knocking.

71 *to be watchers* as having been awake all night

73 *To know my deed ... myself* if I am forced to recognise what I have done, I had better forget who I am (and put on another face or be lost in my thoughts)

> Compare this scene with Act 1 Scene 7, when the murder is planned. In both scenes there is a clear description of what is planned or what is done. Listen for word echoes in the scenes. Has the relationship between the husband and wife changed? Sleep becomes important for both of them in later scenes.

Macbeth returned to his wife in their bedroom. He described the horror of killing the king. Lady Macbeth noticed the guards' bloody daggers in his hand. She took them back to Duncan's room, returned and told Macbeth to change into his nightclothes and wash the blood from his hands.

2:3

The Porter of Macbeth's castle, hung over from the feast, is woken by the knocking of Macduff and Lennox. Lennox describes the unnatural events of the night. Macduff goes to waken the king.

2 *old* plenty of (an outdated use of the word)

4 *Belzebub* the devil/Satan

4–5 *hanged / himself* suicide was a sin, which meant he went to hell

5 *the expectation of plenty* As he had stored extra in order to make a profit in times of shortage, he was devastated when he thought prices were going to go down because of a good harvest. Does this relate to Macbeth's hopes?

5–6 *time-server* someone who adapts opinions and actions to the situation of the moment, as both a farmer and Macbeth do

6 *napkins* towels to wipe away the sweat. This could be suggested by 'server', implying waiter

7 *sweat for't* Hell is burning hot

8 *equivocator* someone who misleads or evades by using ambiguous or unclear language

9–11 *that could swear ... to heaven* Father Garnet tried to lie his way out of being hanged when he was accused of being part of the Gunpowder Plot (see page 5).

13–14 *English tailor ... French hose:* clothing again. French trousers were baggy and English ones took less material

15 *goose* a tailor's smoothing iron; a swelling caused by sexual disease

16 *too cold for hell* traitors are tortured in the frozen circle of hell in Dante's *Inferno*

18 *the primrose way* the pleasant and easy path

48

Get on your nightgown, lest occasion call us   **70**
And show us to be watchers. Be not lost
So poorly in your thoughts.

MACBETH   To know my deed, 'twere best not know myself.   [*Knocking*
Wake Duncan with thy knocking! I would thou couldst.

                                                                [*Exeunt*

2:3   *Knocking within. Enter a* PORTER

PORTER   Here's a knocking indeed! If a man were a porter
of hell-gate, he should have old turning the key.
[*Knocking*] Knock, knock, knock. Who's there, i' th'
name of Belzebub? Here's a farmer, that hanged
himself on the expectation of plenty. Come in time-   **5**
server; have napkins enow about you, here you'll
sweat for't. [*Knocking*] Knock, knock. Who's there, i'
th' other, devil's name? Faith, here's an equivocator,
that could swear in both the scales against either scale;
who committed treason enough for God's sake, yet   **10**
could not equivocate to heaven. O, come in, equivocator.
[*Knocking*] Knock, knock, knock. Who's there?
Faith, here's an English tailor come hither for stealing
out of a French hose. Come in, tailor, here you may
roast your goose. [*Knocking*] Knock, knock. Never at   **15**
quiet! What are you? But this place is too cold for hell.
I'll devil-porter it no further. I had thought to have
let in some of all professions that go the primrose way
to th' everlasting bonfire. [*Knocking*] Anon, anon! I
pray you, remember the porter.   [*Opens the gate   **20**

                        Enter MACDUFF *and* LENNOX

MACDUFF   Was it so late, friend, ere you went to bed,
That you do lie so late?

23   *carousing* partying. *second cock* 3 a.m. By the time of the third cock crow, Judas had betrayed Jesus. Macbeth is about to betray Duncan.

> Either leave the language in the original here or make a modern adaptation. The Porter could wander out from the audience to answer the door of the castle. This is an opportunity to have a good stand-up comic. Some of the best portrayals of drunks happen when the actor shows the character trying hard to appear sober.

30   *equivocator* drink tricks lechery by encouraging it but making it impossible

33–4   *stand to, and not stand to:* both to get and to lose an erection

34   *equivocates him in a sleep* tricks him into going to sleep

35   *giving him the lie* accusing him of lying. This pun, on lies and lying down, is common in other plays.

38   *requited him* paid him back

39   *took up my legs* made me fall down

40   *made a shift to* managed to. *cast* vomit and/or throw him off

41   *thy master* the master of the porter at hell's gate is the devil

44   Macbeth equivocates throughout the scene, intentionally misleading but also speaking truths.

49   *The labour ... pain* because we like what we do, it is no trouble

51   *my limited service* what I have been asked to do

57   *dire combustion* dreadful fires. There is possibly a hint of the Gunpowder Plot here.

58   *obscure bird* the owl, thought to be cursed and to keep to private places

PORTER   Faith, sir, we were carousing till the second cock; and drink, sir, is a
   great provoker of three things.

MACDUFF   What three things does drink especially   **25**
   provoke?

PORTER   Marry, sir, nose-painting, sleep, and urine.
   Lechery, sir, it provokes, and unprovokes: it provokes
   the desire, but it takes away the performance. Therefore
   much drink may be said to be an equivocator   **30**
   with lechery: it makes him, and it mars him; it sets
   him on, and it takes him off; it persuades him, and
   disheartens him; makes him stand to, and not stand
   to, in conclusion, equivocates him in a sleep, and,
   giving him the lie, leaves him.   **35**

MACDUFF   I believe drink gave thee the lie last night.

PORTER   That it did, sir, i' the very throat on me; but I
   requited him for his lie, and I think, being too
   strong for him, though he took up my legs sometime,
   yet I made a shift to cast him.   **40**

MACDUFF   Is thy master stirring?

       Enter MACBETH

   Our knocking has awaked him; here he comes.

LENNOX   Good morrow, noble sir.

MACBETH   Good morrow, both.

MACDUFF   Is the King stirring, worthy Thane?

MACBETH   Not yet.

MACDUFF   He did command me to call timely on him;   **45**
   I have almost slipped the hour.

MACBETH   I'll bring you to him.

MACDUFF   I know this is a joyful trouble to you;
   But yet 'tis one.

MACBETH   The labour we delight in physics pain.
   This is the door.

MACDUFF   I'll make so bold to call,   **50**
   For 'tis my limited service.   *[Exit*

LENNOX   Goes the King hence today?

MACBETH   He does; he did appoint so.

LENNOX   The night has been unruly. Where we lay,
   Our chimneys were blown down, and, as they say,
   Lamentings heard i' th' air; strange screams of death, **55**
   And prophesying, with accents terrible,
   Of dire combustion, and confused events
   New hatched to the woeful time. The obscure bird

60 *feverous and did shake* suffered an earthquake. *'Twas a rough night* Do Macbeth's words show a macabre sense of humour or something else?

> Macbeth's awkwardness and/or breathlessness could be shown here. He might start to go himself to Duncan's door, and then suddenly realise that this is a mistake. His speeches are short but can say much.

67 *The Lord's anointed temple* monarchs were blessed with oil at the coronation to show they were God's choice to rule

71 *Gorgon* mythical Medusa, whose snake-covered head turned anyone who looked at her to stone

75 *death's counterfeit* the imitation of death

77 *The great doom's image* a picture of Doomsday/Judgement Day, the end of the world

78 *walk like sprites* continuing the image of the end of the world when everyone will be spirits

79 *countenance* face

80 *parley* a talk in a situation of war

Clamoured the livelong night. Some say the earth
Was feverous, and did shake.

MACBETH   'Twas a rough night.   60

LENNOX   My young remembrance cannot parallel
A fellow to it.

Enter MACDUFF

MACDUFF   O horror, horror, horror!
Tongue nor heart cannot conceive nor name thee.

MACBETH, LENNOX What's the matter?

MACDUFF Confusion now hath made his masterpiece!   65
Most sacrilegious murder hath broke ope
The Lord's anointed temple, and stole thence
The life o'the building!

MACBETH   What is't you say – the life?

LENNOX   Mean you his Majesty?

MACDUFF   Approach the chamber, and destroy your sight   70
With a new Gorgon. Do not bid me speak;
See, and then speak yourselves.   [*Exeunt MACBETH and LENNOX*
                    Awake, awake!
Ring the alarum-bell. Murder and treason!
Banquo and Donalbain! Malcolm, awake!
Shake off this downy sleep, death's counterfeit,   75
And look on death itself! Up, up, and see
The great doom's image! Malcolm! Banquo!
As from your graves rise up, and walk like sprites,
To countenance this horror!

                                                        [*Bell rings*

Enter LADY MACBETH

LADY MACBETH   What's the business,
That such a hideous trumpet calls to parley   80
The sleepers of the house? Speak, speak!

MACDUFF   O gentle lady,
'Tis not for you to hear what I can speak:
The repetition in a woman's ear
Would murder as it fell.

Enter BANQUO

                    O Banquo, Banquo,
Our royal master's murdered!

LADY MACBETH   Woe, alas!   85
What! in our house?

BANQUO   Too cruel anywhere.
Dear Duff, I prithee contradict thyself,
And say it is not so.

53

89 *Had I but* If I had. *chance* happening

90 *blessed* Macbeth has indeed lost all the blessing in his life, and his life to come.

91 *mortality* human life

93 *drawn* used up. *mere lees* only the dregs

94 *vault* cellar; wine cellar and the cellar-like earth under the roof of the sky, Guy Fawkes' cellar

> *Macbeth's words (lines 89–94) are most often spoken out loud to the company. He could, however, say them as an aside, as he recognises the loss of his own **blessed time** and that his **renown and grace** are dead. Is it possible to speak them out loud, and also imply the terrible recognition of loss for himself?*

106 *temperate* sensible

108 *expedition … love* rush caused by my passionate love. Which 'love' could he mean?

109 *pauser, reason* thinking, which normally delays action

113 *Steeped* Macbeth uses this word later to describe his own guilt

114 *Unmannerly breeched* rudely covered

116 *Courage, to make 's love known?* Lady Macbeth demanded courage as proof of his love for her. *Help me* Editors have usually assumed she faints here but there is no stage direction. She could well be making a distraction for another cause.

119 *argument* subject

120 *hid in an auger-hole* holes made by daggers. Witches also go in and out at auger holes.

124 *Upon the foot of motion* ready to show itself

Here lay Duncan,
His silver skin laced with his golden blood.

Enter MACBETH *and* LENNOX

MACBETH Had I but died an hour before this chance,
I had lived a blessed time; for, from this instant,   90
There's nothing serious in mortality;
All is but toys. Renown and grace is dead,
The wine of life is drawn, and the mere lees
Is left this vault to brag of.

Enter MALCOLM *and* DONALBAIN

DONALBAIN What is amiss?

MACBETH   You are, and do not know't.   95
The spring, the head, the fountain of your blood,
Is stopped; the very source of it is stopped.

MACDUFF Your royal father's murdered.

MALCOLM   O! by whom?

LENNOX   Those of his chamber, as it seemed, had done't:
Their hands and faces were all badged with blood;   100
So were their daggers, which unwiped we found
Upon their pillow. They stared, and were distracted;
No man's life was to be trusted with them.

MACBETH   O yet I do repent me of my fury,
That I did kill them.

MACDUFF   Wherefore did you so?   105

MACBETH   Who can be wise, amazed, temperate and furious,
Loyal and neutral, in a moment? No man.
The expedition of my violent love
Outrun the pauser, reason. Here lay Duncan,
His silver skin laced with his golden blood,   110
And his gashed stabs looked like a breach in nature
For ruin's wasteful entrance; there, the murderers,
Steeped in the colours of their trade, their daggers
Unmannerly breeched with gore. Who could refrain,
That had a heart to love, and in that heart   115
Courage to make 's love known?

LADY MACBETH   Help me hence, ho!

MACDUFF Look to the lady.

MALCOLM [*Aside to* DONALBAIN] Why do we hold our tongues, that most may claim
This argument for ours?

DONALBAIN [*Aside to* MALCOLM] What should be spoken
Here, where our fate, hid in an auger-hole,   120
May rush and seize us? Let's away;
Our tears are not yet brewed.

MALCOLM [*Aside to* DONALBAIN] Nor our strong sorrow
Upon the foot of motion.

128–30 Banquo's oath to make a stand against any hidden plots is taken up by the others. Line 130 is divided between them all. The rhymes *hand, stand* and *thence, pretence* could be a good echo of a witch's evil chant

131 *manly readiness* this means clothing. For Macbeth at this moment could it also mean armour or an innocent-looking face?

133 *consort* join in

138–9 *the near in blood, / The nearer bloody* people who are closely related are dangerous. Macbeth is closely related to Duncan and his sons.

140 *lighted* landed (used of an arrow, for example)

143 *warrant* licence or justification

How can Malcolm and Donalbain have this conversation convincingly, without indicating to the others that they are about to flee secretly?

Compare Macbeth's control of himself in this scene (line 106 onwards) with his uncertainties before he has committed the murder (Act 1 Scene 7, line 31 onwards) and immediately after he has done the deed (Act 2 Scene 2, line 20 onwards).

Lennox and Macduff arrived at the castle to waken Duncan. Macduff finds the king dead. Macbeth pretends anger and stabs the two guards. The thanes and sons then hear the news and Lady Macbeth appears to hear it for the first time. There is general horror and Macbeth speaks of his sadness. The sons plan to flee as they fear for their lives also.

2:4

Ross and an Old Man discuss the unnatural horrors that occurred during the night of the murder. Macduff enters and indicates his view of the events.

1 *Threescore and ten* 70 years

4 *Hath trifled former knowings* made earlier experiences seem like nothing

5 *as* as if they are

5–6 *heavens … act … stage* these refer to features of the Globe theatre (the canopy over the stage was called 'the heavens')

7 *travelling lamp* the sun and/or a carried lantern

8 *Is't night's … shame* is night more powerful, or is the day ashamed to show its face. Day does not come after such a terrible act. After the battle (Act 1 Scene 1) the air, too, is dark. Witches thrive in the dark.

BANQUO   Look to the lady.

LADY MACBETH is carried out

And when we have our naked frailties hid,   **125**
That suffer in exposure, let us meet
And question this most bloody piece of work,
To know it further. Fears and scruples shake us.
In the great hand of God I stand, and thence
Against the undivulged pretence I fight
Of treasonous malice.

MACDUFF   And so do I.

ALL   So all.   **130**

MACBETH   Let's briefly put on manly readiness,
And meet i' the hall together.

ALL   Well contented.

Exeunt all but MALCOLM and DONALBAIN

MALCOLM   What will you do? Let's not consort with them.
To show an unfelt sorrow is an office
Which the false man does easy. I'll to England.   **135**

DONALBAIN To Ireland, I: our separated fortune
Shall keep us both the safer. Where we are
There's daggers in men's smiles – the near in blood,
The nearer bloody.

MALCOLM   This murderous shaft that's shot
Hath not yet lighted, and our safest way   **140**
Is to avoid the aim. Therefore to horse;
And let us not be dainty of leave-taking,
But shift away. There's warrant in that theft
Which steals itself, when there's no mercy left.   [*Exeunt*

2:4   *Enter ROSS and an OLD MAN*

OLD MAN   Threescore and ten I can remember well,
Within the volume of which time I have seen
Hours dreadful, and things strange; but this sore night
Hath trifled former knowings

ROSS   Ha, good father,
Thou seest the heavens, as troubled with man's act,   **5**
Threaten his bloody stage. By the clock 'tis day,
And yet dark night strangles the travelling lamp.
Is't night's predominance, or the day's shame,
That darkness does the face of earth entomb
When living light should kiss it?

17   *contending* arguing

24   *pretend* intend. *suborned* contracted to do a crime

28   *Thriftless* pointless. *ravin up* gobble up (like ravenous or raven-like)

31   *Scone* the royal city, where there was a stone on which Scottish kings were crowned

33   *Colme-kill* Iona, the sacred island where Scottish kings are buried

38   *Lest our old robes … new* the first criticism of Macbeth. Clothing image

40   *benison* blessing

41   *good of bad, and friends of foes.* two antitheses, which perhaps indicate what the Old Man thinks of Ross

Map of Scotland showing places named in the play.

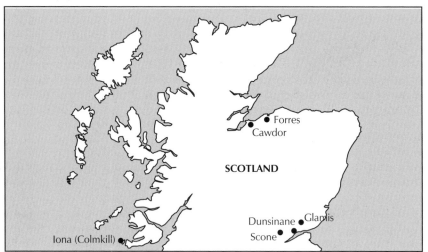

This is the beginning of division in the kingdom: Ross wants to think as well as possible of Macbeth, but Macduff is hugely suspicious of the latter. How does the Old Man fit in? Are these people doing anything – reading a paper or checking in a reference book, looking through a telescope, listening to reports on a radio with earphones?

Compare the weather and strange happenings reported in this scene with the weather and reported happenings of Act 1 Scene 3, lines 1–38 when the witches prophesy.

Ross and the Old Man described horses eating each other and other strange events. Macduff told Ross that the guards were reported to have killed the king, that Macbeth had gone to Scone to be crowned and that Duncan's body had been taken for burial and his sons had fled. Macduff will not attend the coronation.

OLD MAN   'Tis unnatural,   **10**
Even like the deed that's done. On Tuesday last,
A falcon, towering in her pride of place,
Was by a mousing owl hawked at and killed.

ROSS   And Duncan's horses – a thing most strange and certain –
Beauteous and swift, the minions of their race,   **15**
Turned wild in nature, broke their stalls, flung out,
Contending 'gainst obedience, as they would make
War with mankind.

OLD MAN   'Tis said they eat each other.

ROSS   They did so, to the amazement of mine eyes
That looked upon't.
                                   Here comes the good Macduff.   **20**

Enter MACDUFF

How goes the world, sir, now?

MACDUFF   Why, see you not?

ROSS   Is't known who did this more than bloody deed?

MACDUFF   Those that Macbeth hath slain.

ROSS   Alas the day,
What good could they pretend?

MACDUFF   They were suborned.
Malcolm and Donalbain, the King's two sons,   **25**
Are stol'n away and fled, which puts upon them
Suspicion of the deed.

ROSS   'Gainst nature still;
Thriftless ambition, that will ravin up
Thine own life's means! Then 'tis most like
The sovereignty will fall upon Macbeth.   **30**

MACDUFF   He is already named, and gone to Scone
To be invested.

ROSS   Where is Duncan's body?

MACDUFF   Carried to Colme-kill,
The sacred storehouse of his predecessors,
And guardian of their bones.

ROSS   Will you to Scone?   **35**

MACDUFF   No cousin, I'll to Fife.

ROSS   Well, I will thither.

MACDUFF   Well, may you see things well done there – Adieu –
Lest our old robes sit easier than our new!

ROSS   Farewell father.

OLD MAN   God's benison go with you, and with those   **40**
That would make good of bad, and friends of foes.   [*Exeunt*

3:1

Time has passed. Macbeth is king and is holding a formal banquet this evening. Banquo, who privately suspects Macbeth of the murder, is about to go for a ride with Fleance when Macbeth asks about their route. Macbeth, left alone, reveals fear and jealousy of Banquo. He summons two desperate hired killers.

2	*weird* originally the word meant fated or fatal
4	*stand in thy posterity* pass to your sons
5	*root* image of growth
6	*them* the witches
8	*verities* truths
9	*be my oracles* foretell my future. Greek oracles often had double meanings.
10	*But hush, no more* Why does Banquo not speak out?
11–13	*chief guest ... unbecoming* This becomes gruesomely true, although the Macbeths do not know it yet.
13	*all-thing unbecoming* completely inappropriate
14	*we* kings use 'we' instead of 'I'. This is known as the royal plural.
16–18	*indissoluble tie* his oath as a subject of the king. Also their joint experience with the witches *knits* them together. 'Witch' is suggested by the word *which*.
21	*still* always. *prosperous* profitable
22	*tomorrow* a sinister echo of 'tomorrow as he purposes' (Act 1 Scene 5, line 60)
25	*Go not my horse the better* if my horse does not gallop faster than usual
27	*twain* two
31	*parricide* father murder
32	*strange invention* What will Duncan's sons be telling people?
33	*therewithal* along with that
33–4	*cause ... jointly* state business, which needs us both to discuss it
34	*Hie* hurry

3:1   *Enter* **BANQUO**

BANQUO   Thou hast is now, King, Cawdor, Glamis, all,
              As the weird women promised, and I fear
              Thou play'dst most fouly for it; yet it was said
              It should not stand in thy posterity,
              But that myself should be the root and father   5
              Of many kings. If there come truth from them,
              As upon thee, Macbeth, their speeches shine,
              Why, by the verities on thee made good,
              May they not be my oracles as well,
              And set me up in hope? But hush, no more.   10

          Sennet sounded. Enter **MACBETH** *as King,* **LADY MACBETH** *as Queen,*
                  LENNOX, ROSS, LORDS, *and* **ATTENDANTS**

MACBETH   Here's our chief guest.

LADY MACBETH   If he had been forgotten,
              It had been as a gap in our great feast,
              And all-thing unbecoming.

MACBETH   Tonight we hold a solemn supper, sir,
              And I'll request your presence.

BANQUO   Let your Highness   15
              Command upon me, to the which my duties
              Are with a most indissoluble tie
              For ever knit.

MACBETH   Ride you this afternoon?

BANQUO   Ay, my good lord.

MACBETH   We should have else desired your good advice,   20
              Which still hath been both grave and prosperous,
              In this day's council; but we'll take tomorrow.
              Is't far you ride?

BANQUO   As far, my lord, as will fill up the time
              'Twixt this and supper. Go not my horse the better,   25
              I must become a borrower of the night
              For a dark hour or twain.

MACBETH   Fail not our feast.

BANQUO   My lord, I will not.

MACBETH   We hear our bloody cousins are bestowed
              In England and in Ireland, not confessing   30
              Their cruel parricide, filling their hearers
              With strange invention; but of that tomorrow,
              When therewithal we shall have cause of state
              Craving us jointly. Hie you to horse; adieu,
              Till you return at night. Goes Fleance with you?   35

Macbeth

Is Banquo nervous in this conversation? Is he doing anything – putting on his riding boots, tapping his whip impatiently? What is Lady Macbeth doing? She says very little, and is effectively told to leave Macbeth alone. How could you show the development of the relationship here? Are they dressed differently now that they are king and queen?

47–8   *To be thus ... safely thus* to be king in name is nothing unless I am safe on the throne

49   *Stick deep* he may be thinking of daggers and how he killed Duncan

51   *dauntless* fearless. *temper* quality

49–52   *in his royalty ... his valour* Banquo would be a good king. Shakespeare is possibly flattering James I.

55   *Genius is rebuked* natural spirit is overpowered

56   Julius Caesar was a Roman emperor. Mark Antony was his friend of lower rank. *chid* told off

62   *unlineal* someone not in my family line

64   *issue* children and their children. *filed* defiled

66   *rancours* bitterness. *vessel* cup; possibly communion cup

67   *eternal jewel* immortal soul

68   *enemy of man* the devil

69   *seed* image of fruitfulness again

70   *list* field where a tournament was held

71   *to the utterance* to the death (from the French à l'outrance – to the outcome). He is challenging Fate to a fight.

This soliloquy can be played in so many ways. It can be meditative. It can be violent. It can be a mixture. Banquo has just gone out, so he has left a space on the stage. Can this be used in some way to show Macbeth's feelings about Banquo?

73   *yesterday* this suggests he had planned the murder before speaking with Banquo

BANQUO   Ay, my good lord; our time does call upon's.

MACBETH   I wish your horses swift and sure of foot;
And so I do commend you to their backs.
Farewell.   [*Exit* **BANQUO**
Let every man be master of his time   **40**
Till seven at night; to make society
The sweeter welcome, we will keep ourself
Till supper-time alone. While then, God be with you.

[*Exeunt all except* **MACBETH** *and an* **ATTENDANT**

Sirrah, a word with you. Attend those men
Our pleasure?   **45**

ATTENDANT They are, my lord, without the palace gate.

MACBETH   Bring them before us.

[*Exit* **ATTENDANT**

                        To be thus is nothing,
But to be safely thus. Our fears in Banquo
Stick deep; and in his royalty of nature
Reigns that which would be feared. 'Tis much he dares,   **50**
And, to that dauntless temper of his mind,
He hath a wisdom that doth guide his valour
To act in safety. There is none but he
Whose being I do fear; and under him
My Genius is rebuked, as it is said   **55**
Mark Antony's was by Caesar. He chid the sisters
When first they put the name of king upon me,
And bade them speak to him. Then, prophet-like,
They hailed him father to a line of kings.
Upon my head they placed a fruitless crown,   **60**
And put a barren sceptre in my gripe,
Thence to be wrenched with an unlineal hand,
No son of mine succeeding. If't be so,
For Banquo's issue have I filed my mind,
For them the gracious Duncan have I murdered,   **65**
Put rancours in the vessel of my peace
Only for them, and mine eternal jewel
Given to the common enemy of man,
To make them kings, the seed of Banquo kings!
Rather than so, some, fate, into the list,   **70**
And champion me to the utterance. Who's there?

Re-enter **ATTENDANT**, *with two* **MURDERERS**

Now go to the door, and stay there till we call.   [*Exit* **ATTENDANT**
Was it not yesterday we spoke together?

FIRST MURDERER   It was, so please your Highness.

MACBETH   Well then, now

77   *under fortune* below what you deserve

78–9   *This I made good … last conference* Shakespeare does not find it necessary to take the audience through all the details of how Macbeth persuaded the men to become murderers.

79   *passed in probation* went over the proof

80   *borne in hand* manipulated. *crossed* stopped from doing what you wanted, thwarted

82   *half a soul … crazed* to even a madman

87   *gospelled* St Matthew's gospel in the Bible says: 'Doe good to them that hate you, and pray for them which hurt you'.

88   *issue* children

93   *clept* called

94   *valued file* the list which sorts according to value

98   *Hath in him closed* has given to him

99   *Particular addition … bill* special characteristics, as opposed to the list, which makes no distinctions

101   *station in the file* position in this list of men, or file of soldiers

103   *in your bosoms* for you to keep secret and/or to please your hearts

104   *takes … off* kills

105   *Grapples* attaches firmly (as with ships fighting together)

106   *Who wear … life* I feel ill while he is still alive

Have you considered of my speeches? Know
That it was he in the times past which held you
So under fortune, which you thought had been
Our innocent self. This I made good to you
In our last conference, passed in probation with you –
How you were borne in hand, how crossed, the instruments,   **80**
Who wrought with them, and all things else that might
To half a soul and to a notion crazed
Say 'Thus did Banquo'.

First Murderer   You made it known to us.

Macbeth I did so; and went further, which is now
Our point of second meeting. Do you find   **85**
Your patience so predominant in your nature
That you can let this go? Are you so gospelled
To pray for this good man, and for his issue,
Whose heavy hand hath bowed you to the grave,
And beggared yours for ever?

First Murderer   We are men, my liege.   **90**

Macbeth Ay, in the catalogue ye go for men;
As hounds, and greyhounds, mongrels, spaniels, curs,
Shoughs, water-rugs, and demi-wolves are clept
All by the name of dogs. The valued file
Distinguishes the swift, the slow, the subtle,   **95**
The housekeeper, the hunter, every one
According to the gift which bounteous nature
Hath in him closed, whereby he does receive
Particular addition from the bill
That writes them all alike; and so of men.   **100**
Now, if you have a station in the file,
Not i' the worst rank of manhood, say't,
And I will put that business in your bosoms
Whose execution takes your enemy off,
Grapples you to the heart and love of us,   **105**
Who wear our health but sickly in his life,
Which in his death were perfect.

Second Murderer   I am one, my liege,
Whom the vile blows and buffets of the world
Have so incensed that I am reckless what
I do to spite the world.

First Murderer   And I another,   **110**
So weary with disasters, tugged with fortune,
That I would set my life on any chance,
To mend it or be rid on't.

Macbeth   Both of you
Know Banquo was your enemy.

115	*distance* a fencing term meaning the space between opponents
116–17	*every minute … life* every minute he is alive is like a sword thrust
119	*bid my will avouch it* simply justify it by saying it is my wish. Did kings have too much power if they could really do this?
121	*but wail his fall* but I would have to mourn his death
124	*from the common eye* away from public view
126	What do you think the man was going to say?
129	*perfect spy … time* this could mean 'let you know the best time to do it'
131	*something* a little distance away. *always thought* remembering that
132	*I require a clearness* it should seem nothing to do with me
133	*rubs* unevenness
135	*material* important
137	*Resolve yourselves apart* discuss this on your own and make a decision
140–1	Rhyming couplet. What does this show at this point?

The murderers say next to nothing. Notice all the war and fighting imagery. What could they be doing while Macbeth is talking? Why does Shakespeare include this scene? He could have chosen not to. Would you cut it completely, or perhaps shorten it, in performance or is it all important?

Compare this with Act 1 Scene 7, in which Macbeth is struggling with his conscience and his wife over whether to kill Duncan. Why does he take such trouble to justify himself to the men? Does it relate to the trouble he had deciding to murder in the first place?

Macbeth discovered where Banquo was going on his ride and then persuaded two men that they had a grudge against Banquo and that they were not men if they did not want revenge. He employed them to kill Banquo and Fleance that night.

BOTH MURDERERS	True, my lord.	
MACBETH So is he mine; and in such bloody distance		**115**

That every minute of his being thrusts
Against my near'st of life; and though I could
With barefaced power sweep him from my sight,
And bid my will avouch it, yet I must not,
For certain friends that are both his and mine,   **120**
Whose loves I may not drop, but wail his fall
Who I myself struck down. And thence it is
That I to your assistance do make love,
Masking the business from the common eye
For sundry weighty reasons.

SECOND MURDERER   We shall, my lord,   **125**
Perform what you command us.

FIRST MURDERER   Though our lives –

MACBETH Your spirits shine through you. Within this hour, at most,
I will advise you where to plant yourselves,
Acquaint you with the perfect spy o' the time,
The moment on't, for 't must be done tonight,   **130**
And something from the palace; always thought
That I require a clearness – and with him,
To leave no rubs nor botches in the work,
Fleance his son, that keeps him company,
Whose absence is no less material to me   **135**
Than is his father's, must embrace the fate
Of that dark hour. Resolve yourselves apart;
I'll come to you anon.

BOTH MURDERERS   We are resolved, my lord.

MACBETH I'll call upon you straight; abide within.

                                 [Exeunt **MURDERERS**

It is concluded. Banquo, thy soul's flight,   **140**
If it find heaven, must find it out tonight.   *[Exit*

3:2

It is the evening of the formal dinner and Lady Macbeth, unaware of what her husband is planning, is concerned about his behaviour. He has been too much alone recently and has had dreadful nightmares.

1	Is Lady Macbeth suspicious?
4–5	*Nought's had … content* all that we have won is wasted if we cannot enjoy it
7	*doubtful joy* pleasure that is full of suspicion
9	*of sorriest … making* living only with your miserable fantasies
10	*Using* dwelling on
13	*scorched* slashed with a knife. *snake* For Macbeth, evil, or the snake, now lives in Banquo and others who suspect him. So, evil lives in good. (Fair is foul.)
14	*She'll close* the snake (why feminine?) will get her strength back
16–19	*But let … shake us nightly* let the structure of the world fall apart, and both heaven and earth suffer, rather than I should be so afraid and have dreadful dreams
21	*the torture of the mind to lie* the image is of the torture rack
22	*ecstasy* any excitement (joy, sorrow, wonder) that disturbs sanity
23	*fitful* restless. Shakespeare made up this word.
25	*levy* taxation
31	*present him eminence* honour him above all others
32	*Unsafe the while* we are so unsafe. Part of the line may be missing here.
33	*lave* wash or whitewash. *flattering streams* her complimentary words
34	*vizards* masks worn to conceal or protect the face. Here the faces are the masks.
36	*full of scorpions* How does the image fit? Madness? Stinging conscience? Jealousy?

Would you show Lady Macbeth switch, when her husband enters, from her own fear and pain, to an almost motherly comforting of his?

Macbeth is obsessive in his fear, but does not tell her of his plans for Banquo. How could actions show hints of their secret thoughts? Are they being protective of each other? Do they touch each other now?

3:2   *Enter* **Lady Macbeth** *and a* **Servant**

Lady Macbeth   Is Banquo gone from Court?

Servant   Ay, madam, but returns again tonight.

Lady Macbeth   Say to the King, I would attend his leisure.
     For a few words.

Servant   Madam, I will.   [*Exit*

Lady Macbeth   Nought's had, all's spent,
     Where our desire is got without content.   5
     'Tis safer to be that which we destroy
     Than by destruction dwell in doubtful joy.

                   Enter **Macbeth**

     How now, my lord? Why do you keep alone,
     Of sorriest fancies your companions making,
     Using those thoughts which should indeed have died   10
     With them they think on? Things without all remedy
     Should be without regard; what's done is done.

Macbeth   We have scorched the snake, not killed it;
     She'll close, and be herself, whilst our poor malice
     Remains in danger of her former tooth.   15
     But let the frame of things disjoint, both the worlds suffer,
     Ere we will eat our meal in fear, and sleep
     In the affliction of these terrible dreams
     That shake us nightly. Better be with the dead,
     Whom we, to gain our peace, have sent to peace,   20
     Than on the torture of the mind to lie
     In restless ecstasy. Duncan is in his grave;
     After life's fitful fever he sleeps well.
     Treason has done his worst: nor steel, nor poison,
     Malice domestic, foreign levy, nothing   25
     Can touch him further.

Lady Macbeth   Come on;
     Gentle my lord, sleek o'er your rugged looks,
     Be bright and jovial among your guests tonight.

Macbeth   So shall I, love, and so I pray be you.
     Let your remembrance apply to Banquo,   30
     Present him eminence both with eye and tongue –
     Unsafe the while, that we
     Must lave our honours in these flattering streams,
     And make our faces vizards to our hearts,
     Disguising what they are.

Lady Macbeth   You must leave this.   35

Macbeth   O, full of scorpions is my mind, dear wife!
     Thou know'st that Banquo, and his Fleance, lives.

38   *nature's copy's not eterne* they will die and may not leave a copy of themselves. Is she as concerned about children as he is?

39   *they are assailable* they can be reached, or attacked

40   *jocund* playful

40–2   *bat … beetle* note earlier in the scene 'snake … scorpion' and later 'crow … rooky'

41   *cloistered* secret. *Hecate* the witches' queen

42   *shard-borne* carried on scaly wings

42–4   *drowsy hums … yawning peal … dreadful note* sounds of evil. *note* also means fame

46   *seeling* blinding (language of falconry: to sew up the eyes of a hawk to make him obedient)

47   What is *the eye of day*? Why will it be *pitiful*?

49   *that great bond* the human bond, or promise at baptism, that keeps us from committing murder and/or the bond, or promise the witches gave to Banquo

52   *Good things of day begin to droop and drowse* like a headline for the whole scene

54–5   A rhyming couplet. What is its purpose?

Macbeth begins to cheer up his wife. Decide whether you think she knows of his plans to kill Banquo and if so, what she thinks about them. Where is the turning point for Macbeth's mood and how would you show this change? His evil prayer could be accompanied by some sign of the witches' influence. Would some sound be appropriate to accompany **hums, peal** *and* **crow***?*

Compare the invocation to evil in lines 46–54 with Lady Macbeth's prayer for evil assistance in Act 1 Scene 5, lines 40–54. How are the two characters' moods similar in these scenes?

Lady Macbeth tried to comfort Macbeth before the banquet. He was restless and told her to give Banquo special attention. He did not inform her of his plans to have him murdered.

3:3

The murderers wait that evening for Banquo and Fleance. A third murderer joins them unexpectedly, sent by Macbeth. Banquo is killed but Fleance …

S.D.   The third murderer may be there to check up on the other two. Macbeth is very suspicious.

2   *He* refers to either Macbeth or the third murderer. Which fits best?

4   *To the direction just* according to instructions

6   *lated* late. *apace* quickly

5–8   There is, at this point, still light (or life for his soul) for the murderer before he murders Banquo. Macbeth is corrupting others.

LADY MACBETH But in them nature's copy's not eterne.

MACBETH   There's comfort yet; they are assailable.
　　　　Then be thou jocund. Ere the bat hath flown   **40**
　　　　His cloistered flight, ere to black Hecate's summons
　　　　The shard-borne beetle with his drowsy hums
　　　　Hath rung night's yawning peal, there shall be done
　　　　A deed of dreadful note.

LADY MACBETH   What's to be done?

MACBETH   Be innocent of the knowledge, dearest chuck,   **45**
　　　　Till thou applaud the deed. Come, seeling night,
　　　　Scarf up the tender eye of pitiful day,
　　　　And with thy bloody and invisible hand
　　　　Cancel and tear to pieces that great bond
　　　　Which keeps me pale. Light thickens, and the crow   **50**
　　　　Makes wing to the rooky wood.
　　　　Good things of day begin to droop and drowse,
　　　　Whiles night's black agents to their preys do rouse.
　　　　Thou marvell'st at my words; but hold thee still,
　　　　Things bad begun make strong themselves by ill.   **55**
　　　　So, prithee, go with me.   [*Exeunt*

3:3   *Enter three* MURDERERS

FIRST MURDERER   But who did bid thee join with us?

THIRD MURDERER   Macbeth.

SECOND MURDERER He needs not our mistrust, since he delivers
　　　　Our offices, and what we have to do,
　　　　To the direction just.

FIRST MURDERER   Then stand with us,
　　　　The west yet glimmers with some streaks of day;   **5**
　　　　Now spurs the lated traveller apace

8	*horses* These are heard but not seen, at least on stage.
10	*within the note of expectation* on the guest list for the banquet
11–14	The horses are taken to the back of the castle and Banquo and Fleance walk by a shorter route.

Would you have the actors perform this visibly or would you have a complete blackout, so that the audience cannot see anything of the murder, and rely totally on sounds to create the drama of the scene?

Compare this murder with the murder of Duncan. Consider the build-up to the murder, the characters involved, the changes evident in Macbeth's attitude and approach, and the setting chosen by Shakespeare.

Banquo is murdered by the roadside but Fleance escaped unhurt.

    To gain the timely inn, and near approaches
    The subject of our watch.

THIRD MURDERER   Hark! I hear horses.

BANQUO [*Within*]   Give us a light there, ho!

SECOND MURDERER   Then 'tis he. The rest
    That are within the note of expectation   **10**
    Already are i' the court.

FIRST MURDERER   His horses go about.

THIRD MURDERER   Almost a mile; but he does usually,
    So all men do, from hence to the palace gate
    Make it their walk.

             Enter **BANQUO** *and* **FLEANCE**, *with a torch*

SECOND MURDERER   A light, a light!

THIRD MURDERER   'Tis he.

FIRST MURDERER   Stand to't.   **15**

BANQUO   It will be rain tonight.

FIRST MURDERER   Let it come down.

      First Murderer strikes out the torch, and they attack **BANQUO** *and* **FLEANCE**

BANQUO   O treachery! Fly, good Fleance, fly, fly, fly!
    Thou mayst revenge – O slave!

                BANQUO *falls;* **FLEANCE** *escapes*

THIRD MURDERER   Who did strike out the light?

FIRST MURDERER   Was't not the way?

THIRD MURDERER   There's but one down; the son is fled.

SECOND MURDERER   We have lost   **20**
    Best half of our affair.

FIRST MURDERER   Well, let's away,
    And say how much is done.   [*Exeunt*

3:4

Macbeth and his wife, now king and queen, are holding a banquet for their thanes. The murderers tell Macbeth that Banquo is dead but Fleance has escaped. Macbeth tries to sit at the table, but cannot, because the ghost of Banquo appears.

1	*degrees* rank, position of importance compared with other guests
1–2	*at first / And last* whatever rank you are
3–6	Macbeth uses the royal plural three times in this short speech.
5	*state* a chair of state
10	*Both sides are even* either: the guests are sitting in equal numbers on both sides of the table; or: the guests have returned thanks for her welcome
11	*large* free. *anon* soon

How would you set the table? Is there a tablecloth? What colour is it? What is on the table? How many guests and serving people are there? Would it be appropriate to spend time creating a party mood with music and drinks etc? Would an interval between scenes 3 and 4 be appropriate? What would it achieve?

14	It is better on your outside than inside him. Should it be said with relief or as a joke?
15	*dispatched* dealt with/killed
18	*nonpareil* unmatched
21	*founded* immovable
22	*As broad … air* as free and unrestrained as the air around us
23	*cribbed* shut into a small space
26	*trenched* deeply cut
27	*The least* even the smallest one
28	*worm* young serpent. Another reference to other snakes and scorpions.
31	*hear ourselves* speak together. *ourselves* refers to the murderers and Macbeth also.
32	*the cheer* the toast
32–4	*the feast is sold … welcome* you may as well charge money for the feast if you do not keep saying that the guests are welcome

Does Macbeth sound relaxed? Is he a good host? What mood do you think the guests would be in at the beginning of the banquet?

It can be difficult on stage to continue with the party and at the same time hear Macbeth's discussion with the murderers. How would you achieve this? For example, Macbeth and the murderers come forward; the guests freeze in a silent tableau; the guests mime.

3:4   *A banquet prepared. Enter* Macbeth, Lady Macbeth, Ross,
Lennox, Lords, *and* Attendants

Macbeth   You know your own degrees, sit down. At first
And last, the hearty welcome.

Lords   Thanks to your Majesty.

Macbeth   Ourself will mingle with society,
And play the humble host.
Our hostess keeps her state, but in best time   5
We will require her welcome.

Lady Macbeth   Pronounce it for me, sir, to all our friends,
For my heart speaks they are welcome.

                 Enter First Murderer, *to the door*

Macbeth   See, they encounter thee with their hearts' thanks.
Both sides are even; here I'll sit i' the midst.   10
Be large in mirth; anon we'll drink a measure
The table round.   *[Goes to the door*
There's blood upon thy face.

Murderer   'Tis Banquo's then.

Macbeth   'Tis better thee without than he within.
Is he dispatched?

Murderer   My lord, his throat is cut;   15
That I did for him.

Macbeth   Thou art the best o' the cut-throats;
Yet he's good that did the like for Fleance.
If thou didst it, thou art the nonpareil.

Murderer   Most royal sir, – Fleance is 'scaped.

Macbeth   Then comes my fit again. I had else been perfect;   20
Whole as the marble, founded as the rock,
As broad and general as the casing air;
But now I am cabined, cribbed, confined, bound in
To saucy doubts and fears. But Banquo's safe?

Murderer   Ay, my good lord; safe in a ditch he bides,   25
With twenty trenched gashes on his head,
The least a death to nature.

Macbeth   Thanks for that.
There the grown serpent lies; the worm that's fled
Hath nature that in time will venom breed,
No teeth for the present. Get thee gone; tomorrow   30
We'll hear ourselves again.   *[Exit* Murderer

Lady Macbeth   My royal lord,
You do not give the cheer. The feast is sold
That is not often vouched, while 'tis a-making,

35 *From thence* if away from home

35–6 *meat … Meeting* this is a pun

36 *remembrancer* reminder

39 *roofed* complete under one roof

41 *mischance* an accident

42 *moves* upsets

49 *Thou canst not say I did it* Technically, he did not commit the murder.

50 *gory locks* bloody strands of hair

56 *extend his passion* prolong his suffering

61 *which you said* Macbeth must have told her about the visionary dagger

62 *flaws* gusts of passion

'Tis given with welcome. To feed were best at home;
From thence, the sauce to meat is ceremony; 35
Meeting were bare without it.

MACBETH   Sweet remembrancer!
Now good digestion wait on appetite,
And health on both.

LENNOX   May't please your Highness sit.

MACBETH   Here had we now our country's honour roofed,
Were the graced person of our Banquo present; 40

The GHOST *of* BANQUO *enters, and sits in* MACBETH'S *place*

Who may I rather challenge for unkindness
Than pity for mischance.

ROSS   His absence, sir,
Lays blame upon his promise. Please 't your Highness
To grace us with your royal company?

MACBETH   The table's full.

LENNOX   Here is a place reserved, sir. 45

MACBETH   Where?

LENNOX   Here, my good lord. – What is't that moves your Highness?

MACBETH   Which of you have done this?

LORDS   What, my good lord?

MACBETH [*To the* GHOST] Thou canst not say I did it; never shake
Thy gory locks at me. 50

ROSS   Gentlemen, rise; his Highness is not well.

LADY MACBETH   Sit, worthy friends. My lord is often thus,
And hath been from his youth. Pray you, keep seat;
The fit is momentary, upon a thought
He will again be well. If much you note him, 55
You shall offend him and extend his passion.
Feed, and regard him not. [*To* MACBETH] Are you a man?

MACBETH   Ay, and a bold one, that dare look on that
Which might appal the devil.

LADY MACBETH   O proper stuff!
This is the very painting of your fear. 60
This is the air-drawn dagger which you said
Led you to Duncan. O, these flaws and starts,
Impostors to true fear, would well become
A woman's story at a winter's fire,
Authorised by her grandam. Shame itself! 65
Why do you make such faces? When all's done,
You look but on a stool.

MACBETH   Prithee, see there!

70   *charnel-houses* burial places for bones from reused graves

72   *maws of kites* mouths of birds of prey (which vomit up undigested food)

> When would the Ghost enter and what would he look like? What would be more effective for the Ghost: a) to use the actor playing Banquo; b) to not have an actor, so the audience and guests do not see anything; c) to use sound effects or lighting only?
>
> Lady Macbeth is like a parent or teacher to a child here. Would she be indulgent and kindly, very angry, spittingly scornful or just amazed and bewildered?

75   *Ere humane … weal* before laws made people more civilised

80   *twenty mortal murders* compare line 26

83   *lack* miss

90   *and him, we thirst* we long for him like thirsting for a drink

91   *the pledge* the toast to Banquo that Macbeth has just made

94   *speculation* understanding

100 *armed rhinoceros* its hide was like armour. *Hyrcan* from the Caspian Sea

104 *If trembling I inhabit then* if I tremble then. *protest me* say I am like

Come, love and health to all.

Behold! look! lo! How say you?
Why, what care I! If thou canst nod, speak too.
If charnel-houses and our graves must send   70
Those that we bury back, our monuments
Shall be the maws of kites.   [*Exit* GHOST

LADY MACBETH   What, quite unmanned in folly?

MACBETH   If I stand here, I saw him.

LADY MACBETH   Fie, for shame!

MACBETH   Blood hath been shed ere now, i' the olden time,
Ere humane statute purged the gentle weal;   75
Ay, and since too, murders have been performed
Too terrible for the ear. The time has been
That when the brains were out the man would die,
And there an end. But now they rise again,
With twenty mortal murders on their crowns,   80
And push us from our stools. This is more strange
Than such a murder is.

LADY MACBETH   My worthy lord,
Your noble friends do lack you.

MACBETH   I do forget.
Do not muse at me, my most worthy friends;
I have a strange infirmity, which is nothing   85
To those that know me. Come, love and health to all;
Then I'll sit down. Give me some wine; fill full.
I drink to the general joy o' the whole table,
And to our dear friend Banquo, whom we miss;

Enter GHOST

Would he were here! To all, and him, we thirst,   90
And all to all.

LORDS   Our duties, and the pledge.

MACBETH [*To the* GHOST] Avaunt, and quit my sight! Let the earth hide thee!
Thy bones are marrowless, thy blood is cold;
Thou hast no speculation in those eyes
Which thou dost glare with!

LADY MACBETH   Think of this, good peers,   95
But as a thing of custom. 'Tis no other;
Only it spoils the pleasure of the time.

MACBETH   What man dare, I dare.
Approach thou like the rugged Russian bear,
The armed rhinoceros, or the Hyrcan tiger,   100
Take any shape but that, and my firm nerves
Shall never tremble. Or be alive again,
And dare me to the desert with thy sword;
If trembling I inhabit then, protest me

105 *the baby of a girl* a girl's doll

109 *admired* amazing; so that people are all looking at you

111–12 *make me strange ... owe* make me feel I do not know myself

117 *Question enrages him* What danger does Lady Macbeth sense here?

118 *Stand not ... going* do not go out in order of your ranks (as they would normally do after a feast)

Does the Ghost come in at the same place as before?
Does Macbeth reach for a weapon when he sees it again?
Would you use objects on the table or on a sideboard to emphasise the movements of any of the characters? How could Ross say
What sights, my lord? *Would it have a different tone from Lennox earlier,* **What is't that moves your highness?**

123 *Augures* foretelling the future. *understood relations* knowing what augurs mean

124 *magot-pies* magpies. *choughs* crows. *brought forth* revealed

125 *the secret'st man of blood* the most hidden murderer

126 *Almost ... which* This is a turning point between night and day. Banquo is dead. Macduff is coming.

130–1 *There's not a one ... fee'd* I keep a servant, paid as a spy, in all the thanes' houses

135 *All causes shall give way* all other thoughts and jobs will take second place to this

135–7 *I am in blood ... as tedious as go o'er* I have waded so far in blood (as in a river) that it would be as difficult to go back as to go forward. This is the halfway point in the play.

138 *that will to hand* that must be done

139 *scanned* seen. This is a rhyming couplet. What is its effect?

The baby of a girl. Hence, horrible shadow! 105
Unreal mockery, hence! [*Exit* **Ghost**
                    Why, so; being gone,
I am a man again. [*To the* **Lords**] Pray you, sit still.

Lady Macbeth You have displaced the mirth, broke the good meeting
    With most admired disorder.

Macbeth   Can such things be,
    And overcome us like a summer's cloud, 110
    Without our special wonder? You make me strange
    Even to the disposition that I owe,
    When now I think you can behold such sights
    And keep the natural ruby of your cheeks,
    When mine is blanched with fear.

Ross   What sights, my lord? 115

Lady Macbeth I pray you, speak not. He grows worse and worse;
    Question enrages him. At once, good night.
    Stand not upon the order of you going,
    But go at once.

Lennox   Good night; and better health
    Attend his Majesty.

Lady Macbeth   A kind good night to all. 120

            Exeunt all but **Macbeth** *and* **Lady Macbeth**

Macbeth   It will have blood, they say; blood will have blood.
    Stones have been known to move, and trees to speak;
    Augures and understood relations have
    By magot-pies and choughs and rooks brought forth
    The secret'st man of blood. What is the night? 125

Lady Macbeth Almost at odds with morning, which is which.

Macbeth   How say'st thou, that Macduff denies his person
    At our great bidding?

Lady Macbeth   Did you send to him, sir?

Macbeth   I hear it by the way; but I will send.
    There's not a one of them but in his house 130
    I keep a servant fee'd. I will tomorrow,
    (And betimes I will) to the Weird Sisters.
    More shall they speak; for now I am bent to know
    By the worst means the worst. For mine own good
    All causes shall give way. I am in blood 135
    Stepped in so far that, should I wade no more,
    Returning were as tedious as go o'er.
    Strange things I have in head that will to hand,
    Which must be acted ere they may be scanned.

Lady Macbeth You lack the season of all natures, sleep. 140

81

141 *strange and self-abuse* this unusual pain I am suffering

142 *initiate fear* the fear of a beginner. *that wants hard use* who does not have regular experience of doing evil to toughen him up

143 *young in deed* inexperienced in doing wrong

> Lady Macbeth can be played in a variety of ways here. Do you think she would be the efficient hostess, or completely worn out and confused by her husband, or something else? Is he going mad? How could you show his state of mind? In his gestures, in his voice and movements?

Compare this banquet with the earlier banquet, before Macbeth has murdered Duncan (Act 1 Scene 7). How are they alike and how unlike?

During the banquet Macbeth heard that Banquo had been successfully murdered. He then tried to sit at the table but kept seeing the ghost of Banquo in the seat. He showed his terror to the guests, who could not see the ghost. Lady Macbeth tried to cover up for him and told the guests to leave quickly.

Lady Macbeth in despair after everyone has left the banquet.

3:5

The witches meet again in thunder. Hecate, their goddess, is angry because they did not involve her in the destruction of Macbeth. We now see her huge powers (greater than those of the other witches) as she continues his bewitchment. She conjures up spirits to induce a misleading sense of security in Macbeth.

It has been thought that Shakespeare did not write this scene himself but there is no clear evidence one way or the other. Conjuring scenes, with devil-like performers, were popular in the theatre of the time. It is written in the four-beat chant-like rhythm that the witches have used before.

2 *beldams* old women

MACBETH   Come, we'll to sleep. My strange and self-abuse
    Is the initiate fear that wants hard use:
    We are yet but young in deed.

                                              [*Exeunt*

3:5   *Thunder. Enter the three* WITCHES, *meeting* HECATE

FIRST WITCH   Why, how now, Hecate? You look angerly.

HECATE   Have I not reason, beldams as you are,
    Saucy and overbold? How did you dare
    To trade and traffic with Macbeth
    In riddles and affairs of death;   5
    And I, the mistress of your charms,
    The close contriver of all harms,
    Was never called to bear my part,
    Or show the glory of our art?
    And, which is worse, all you have done   10
    Hath been but for a wayward son,

Macbeth

Your vessels and your spells provide,
Your charms, and every thing beside.

15 *Acheron* a river in the underworld of Greek mythology

16–17 *Thither he / Will come* He has just said he will to his wife. Did Hecate hear this or does she really know the future?

21 *dismal* disastrous

26 *sleights* tricks

27 *sprites* spirit visions. (She does indeed conjure up apparitions for Macbeth to see.)

32 *security* too much confidence and/or a bond or pact with the devil

> *Hecate gives an opportunity for developing the dramatic presentation of the witches. In what ways could you use music, dance, or sound effects? Consider whether Hecate, or one of the other witches, should be reminiscent of Lady Macbeth.*

Compare this with Act 1 scenes 1 and 3, the only other times we have seen the witches in the play so far. How have they developed as characters? In what ways does Shakespeare maintain or increase the audience's interest in them?

3:6

Lennox and a lord meet to discuss their suspicion and hatred of Macbeth. The lord informs him that Malcolm is in England and Macduff has gone to meet him there.

1 *former speeches* he has spoken with the lord before.
hit coincided with

3 *borne* done

7 *Men must not walk too late* Lennox is being cautious

8 *Who cannot want the thought* Everybody must think

Spiteful and wrathful, who, as others do,
Loves for his own ends, not for you.
But make amends now; get you gone,
And at the pit of Acheron   15
Meet me i' the morning. Thither he
Will come to know his destiny,
Your vessels and your spells provide,
Your charms, and every thing beside.
I am for th' air; this night I'll spend   20
Unto a dismal and a fatal end.
Great business must be wrought ere noon:
Upon the corner of the moon
There hangs a vap'rous drop profound;
I'll catch it ere it come to ground;   25
And that, distilled by magic sleights,
Shall raise such artificial sprites
As, by the strength of their illusion,
Shall draw him on to his confusion.
He shall spurn fate, scorn death, and bear   30
His hopes 'bove wisdom, grace, and fear;
) And you all know security
Is mortal's chiefest enemy.
[*Music and a song within*, 'Come away, come away,' etc.]
Hark! I am call'd; my little spirit, see,
Sits in a foggy cloud, and stays for me.   [*Exit*   35

First Witch   Come, let's make haste; she'll soon be back again.   [*Exeunt*

3:6   *Enter* **Lennox** *and another* **Lord**

Lennox   My former speeches have but hit your thoughts,
Which can interpret further; only I say
Things have been strangely borne. The gracious Duncan
Was pitied of Macbeth – marry, he was dead;
And the right-valiant Banquo walked too late –   5
Whom you may say, if't please you, Fleance killed,
For Fleance fled. Men must not walk too late.
Who cannot want the thought how monstrous
It was for Malcolm and for Donalbain
To kill their gracious father? Damned fact!   10
How did it grieve Macbeth! Did he not straight
In pious rage the two delinquents tear,
That were the slaves of drink and thralls of sleep?

18	*had he*	if he had
21	*broad words*	rumours abroad
25	*holds the due of birth*	witholds his right to the throne as the son of Duncan
28	*the malevolence of fortune*	his bad luck in the world
30	*upon his aid*	for his help
32–3	*with Him above/To ratify the work*	with God to justify what is done
38	*he*	It is not clear whether this means the English king or Macbeth.
42–3	*You'll rue … answer*	you'll regret asking me to tell him that
45–7	*Some holy angel … come*	He wishes someone would tell the English king that Macduff is coming to get help.

The two men would very likely meet in secret. Where would be an appropriate place? They may, however, not be alone but only speak secretly together. They could whisper together at some sort of business meeting or social engagement.

Compare the descriptions of Macbeth here with the glowing praises of him spoken by Duncan, Ross and the Captain in Act 1 Scene 2.

Lennox and a lord longed for peace to return to Scotland, which has been suffering greatly under Macbeth. Malcolm had asked the king of England for military help against Macbeth.

Was not that nobly done? Ay, and wisely too;
For 'twould have angered any heart alive 15
To hear the men deny't. So that, I say,
He has borne all things well; and I do think
That had he Duncan's sons under his key
(As, an't please heaven, he shall not) they should find
What 'twere to kill a father; so should Fleance. 20
But peace – for from broad words, and 'cause he failed
His presence at the tyrant's feast, I hear
Macduff lives in disgrace. Sir, can you tell
Where he bestows himself?

LORD   The son of Duncan
From whom this tyrant holds the due of birth, 25
Lives in the English Court, and is received
Of the most pious Edward with such grace
That the malevolence of fortune nothing
Takes from his high respect. Thither Macduff
Is gone to pray the holy King, upon his aid 30
To wake Northumberland and warlike Siward,
That by the help of these, with Him above
To ratify the work, we may again
Give to our tables meat, sleep to our nights,
Free from our feasts and banquets bloody knives, 35
Do faithful homage, and receive free honours –
All which we pine for now. And this report
Hath so exasperate the King that he
Prepares for some attempt of war.

LENNOX   Sent he to Macduff?

LORD   He did; and with an absolute 'Sir, not I' 40
The cloudy messenger turns me his back,
And hums, as who should say, 'You'll rue the time
That clogs me with this answer'.

LENNOX   And that well might
Advise him to a caution, to hold what distance
His wisdom can provide. Some holy angel 45
Fly to the court of England and unfold
His message ere he come, that a swift blessing
May soon return to this our suffering country
Under a hand accursed.

LORD   I'll send my prayers with him.

                                      [*Exeunt*

4:1

A group of witches prepare a cauldron of charms to influence Macbeth. He arrives to ask for further predictions. They spirit up a series of visions with messages about the future. Thunder accompanies the preparation of the cauldron and the visions.

1   *Thrice* Once again the number three is connected with witches. *brinded* with streaked fur

2   *hedge-pig* hedgehog

3   *Harpier* a witch's familiar (a harpy is a flying spirit with a woman's face)

8   *Sweltered venom* sweated poison

10   *Double* continues the idea of two sides to everything. The rhyme is also in twos. This amplifies the chant-like rhythm. There are four beats in the lines for the witches' chant.

12   *Fillet of a fenny snake* slice of a snake from bogs or fens

16   *Adder's fork* this poisonous snake has a forked (double) tongue. *blind-worm* slow-worm (thought, like the newt, to be poisonous but now known to be harmless)

17   *howlet* young owl

23–5   Notice the alliteration (repetition of consonant sounds) in these chants.

23   *mummy* juices from mummified bodies (also used in medicine). *maw and gulf* mouth and stomach

24   *ravined* fully fed

25   *hemlock digged i' the dark* a herb, supposedly more poisonous for being dug up at night

26–9   *Jew … Turk … Tartar* non-Christian and therefore unbaptised. Witches used parts of unconsecrated bodies.

27   *yew* poisonous tree, planted in churchyards. Its red berries look like drops of blood.

28   *slivered* sliced off

31   *drab* prostitute. Her baby would be unbaptised.

33   *chaudron* entrails

4:1   *Thunder. Enter the three* WITCHES

FIRST WITCH   Thrice the brinded cat hath mewed.

SECOND WITCH Thrice and once the hedge-pig whined.

THIRD WITCH   Harpier cries – 'Tis time, 'tis time.

FIRST WITCH   Round about the cauldron go;
In the poisoned entrails throw.   5
Toad, that under cold stone
Days and nights hast thirty-one
Sweltered venom sleeping got,
Boil thou first i' th' charmed pot.

ALL   Double, double, toil and trouble;   10
Fire burn, and cauldron bubble.

SECOND WITCH Fillet of a fenny snake,
In the cauldron boil and bake;
Eye of newt, and toe of frog,
Wool of bat, and tongue of dog,   15
Adder's fork, and blind-worm's sting,
Lizard's leg, and howlet's wing,
For a charm of powerful trouble,
Like a hell-broth boil and bubble.

ALL   Double, double, toil and trouble;   20
Fire burn, and cauldron bubble.

THIRD WITCH   Scale of dragon, tooth of wolf,
Witches' mummy, maw and gulf
Of the ravined salt-sea shark,
Root of hemlock digged i' the dark,   25
Liver of blaspheming Jew,
Gall of goat, and slips of yew
Slivered in the moon's eclipse,
Nose of Turk, and Tartar's lips,
Finger of birth-strangled babe   30
Ditch-delivered by a drab,
Make the gruel thick and slab;
Add thereto a tiger's chaudron,
For th' ingredience of our cauldron.

ALL   Double, double, toil and trouble;   35
Fire burn, and cauldron bubble.

SECOND WITCH Cool it with a baboon's blood,
Then the charm is firm and good.

44 *pricking of my thumbs* unusual pains foretold that something was going to happen

47 *knocks* Macbeth's heart knocked (Act 1 Scene 3, line 136) when he first thought of murder. He heard knocking (Act 2 Scene 2, line 57) when he had just committed the murder.

> *Rhythm, rhyme, dance/movement, and voice create the effectiveness of this scene. The cauldron is filled with animal parts. Could you get the effect of live animals by using sound and flurries of movement with materials? This scene needs to be tried out in different ways in groups, using varying pitches of sound and voice, sound in unison and harmony, and so on. One witch coming out from the audience clutching a finger of a* **birth-strangled babe** *could add some horror.*

48 *black* practising black magic

51 *Howe'er you come to know it* even if by evil, ie making a pact with the devil

53 *Against the churches* against good, and against church buildings. *yesty* frothing

55 *lodged* flattened

59 *nature's germens* good seeds of nature for reproduction and health. Macbeth is prepared to risk the destruction of the whole world as long as he can know his future.

65 *nine* three x three again. *farrow* litter of piglets (another unnatural mother). *grease* sweat

66 *From the murderer's gibbet* from the gallows on which a murderer had been hanged

Enter **HECATE** *and the other three* **WITCHES**

HECATE   O, well done! I commend your pains,
        And every one shall share i' th' gains.   40
        And now about the cauldron sing,
        Like elves and fairies in a ring,
        Enchanting all that you put in.
        Music and a song, 'Black spirits,' etc.

                [*Exeunt* **HECATE** *and the other three* **WITCHES**

SECOND WITCH By the pricking of my thumbs,
        Something wicked this way comes: 45
        Open, locks,
        Whoever knocks.

                Enter **MACBETH**

MACBETH   How now, you secret, black, and midnight hags!
        What is't you do?

ALL   A deed without a name.

MACBETH   I conjure you by that which you profess –   50
        Howe'er you come to know it – answer me.
        Though you untie the winds and let them fight
        Against the churches; though the yesty waves
        Confound and swallow navigation up;
        Though bladed corn be lodged, and trees blown down;   55
        Though castles topple on their warders' heads;
        Though palaces and pyramids do slope
        Their heads to their foundations; though the treasure
        Of nature's germens tumble all together,
        Even till destruction sicken – answer me   60
        To what I ask you.

FIRST WITCH   Speak.

SECOND WITCH   Demand.

THIRD WITCH   We'll answer.

FIRST WITCH   Say if thou'dst rather hear it from our mouths,
        Or from our masters?

MACBETH   Call 'em, let me see 'em.

FIRST WITCH   Pour in sow's blood, that hath eaten
        Her nine farrow; grease that's sweaten   65
        From the murderer's gibbet, throw
        Into the flame.

ALL   Come high or low;
        Thyself and office deftly show.

                Thunder. **FIRST APPARITION,** *an Armed Head*

70   *say thou nought* characters in plays were often told to keep silent when confronted with spirits

74   *harped* guessed or given voice to

76   *potent* powerful

78   *three* yet again

84   *take a bond of fate* he does not trust fate and needs to make absolutely sure. *Thou* Macduff

86   *sleep* remember Macbeth feels he has murdered sleep

87–8   *issue … baby* Macbeth's concern with inheritance

88–9   *round / And top of sovereignty* the crown

93   *Dunsinane* a Scottish castle near Perth, and on a hill, so good for defence

95–101   Macbeth echoes the rhyme of the apparitions, linking himself with these spirits

97   *Rebellious dead* Macbeth may still be remembering Banquo's ghost

99   *lease of nature* normal span of life

100   *mortal custom* natural death (not in battle)

MACBETH	Tell me, thou unknown power –
FIRST WITCH	He knows thy thought;

Hear his speech, but say thou nought.   70

FIRST APPARITION Macbeth, Macbeth, Macbeth! Beware Macduff;
Beware the Thane of Fife. Dismiss me. Enough.

[Descends

MACBETH   Whate'er thou art, for thy good caution thanks;
Thou hast harped my fear aright. But one word more –

FIRST WITCH   He will not be commanded. Here's another,   75
More potent than the first.

Thunder. **SECOND APPARITION,** *a Bloody Child*

SECOND APPARITION Macbeth, Macbeth, Macbeth!

MACBETH   Had I three ears, I'd hear thee.

SECOND APPARITION Be bloody, bold, and resolute; laugh to scorn
The power of man, for none of woman born   80
Shall harm Macbeth.

[Descends

MACBETH   Then live, Macduff; what need I fear of thee?
But yet I'll make assurance double sure,
And take a bond of fate. Thou shalt not live,
That I may tell pale-hearted fear it lies,   85
And sleep in spite of thunder.

Thunder. **THIRD APPARITION,** *a Child Crowned, with a Tree in his Hand*

What is this,
That rises like the issue of a king,
And wears upon his baby brow the round
And top of sovereignty?

ALL   Listen, but speak not to't.

THIRD APPARITION Be lion-mettled, proud, and take no care   90
Who chafes, who frets, or where conspirers are.
Macbeth shall never vanquished be until
Great Birnam wood to high Dunsinane hill
Shall come against him.   *[Descends*

MACBETH   That will never be:
Who can impress the forest, bid the tree   95
Unfix his earth-bound root? Sweet bodements, good!
Rebellious dead, rise never till the wood
Of Birnam rise; and our high-placed Macbeth
Shall live the lease of nature, pay his breath
To time and mortal custom. Yet my heart   100
Throbs to know one thing: tell me, if your art
Can tell so much, shall Banquo's issue ever
Reign in this kingdom?

104–5 *Deny me … curse fall on you* he uses a demonic curse to force them

106 *sinks … noise* indications of the staging of Shakespeare's play

> There was a trapdoor under the stage in Shakespeare's time, so it is possible that **sinks** could mean that the apparitions came from under the stage. How would you do them now? Macbeth's exclamation **what noise is this** implies a loud sound effect at this point.

S.D. The show of kings with Banquo at the end reveals to Macbeth the line of kings, stemming from Banquo, that has continued until the accession of James I.

113 *hair* Does this also imply heir, do you think? A pun.

119 *eighth* there were eight kings from Banquo to James I.
glass mirror

121 *twofold balls and treble sceptres* usually thought to refer to James I, who as well as being king of Scotland became king of England at this time

127 *sprites* spirits, meaning to cheer him up after the visions of the kings of Scotland. They did not want him to see that but he forced them with his curse (line 105).

130 *antic round* fantastic dance

134 *aye* forever

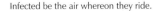

Infected be the air whereon they ride.

ALL	Seek to know no more.
MACBETH	I will be satisfied. Deny me this,

And an eternal curse fall on you! Let me know. –   105
Why sinks that cauldron, and what noise is this?

[*Hautboys*

FIRST WITCH	Show!
SECOND WITCH	Show!
THIRD WITCH	Show!
ALL	Show his eyes, and grieve his heart; 110

Come like shadows, so depart.

A show of eight **KINGS**, *the last with a Glass in his hand;*
the **GHOST** *of* **BANQUO** *following*

MACBETH   Thou art too like the spirit of Banquo; down!
Thy crown does sear mine eyeballs. And thy hair,
Thou other gold-bound brow, is like the first. –
A third is like the former. Filthy hags!   115
Why do you show me this? A fourth? Start, eyes!
What, will the line stretch out to the crack of doom?
Another yet? A seventh? I'll see no more;
And yet the eighth appears, who bears a glass
Which shows me many more; and some I see   120
That twofold balls and treble sceptres carry.
Horrible sight! Now I see 'tis true,
For the blood-boltered Banquo smiles upon me,
And points at them for his. What! is this so?

FIRST WITCH   Ay, sir, all this is so. But why   125
Stands Macbeth thus amazedly?
Come, sisters, cheer we up his sprites,
And show the best of our delights.
I'll charm the air to give a sound,
While you perform your antic round,   130
That this great king may kindly say
Our duties did his welcome pay.

Music. The **WITCHES** *dance, and vanish*

MACBETH   Where are they? Gone? Let this pernicious hour
Stand aye accursèd in the calendar!
Come in, without there!   135

Enter **LENNOX**

LENNOX	What's your Grace's will?
MACBETH	Saw you the Weird Sisters?
LENNOX	No, my lord.

139 *damned* Macbeth does trust them and is damned

144 *anticipat'st my dread exploits* you see beforehand the terrible deeds I have planned

145–6 *flighty purpose … with it* the speedy intention is never completed unless it is done as soon as thought

But no more sights. *How should Macbeth say this line? A gesture could recall the dagger vision perhaps.*

Compare this scene with the first occasion when he meets the witches (Act 1 Scene 3). How is his attitude different now? Also compare the vision of the dagger before he kills Duncan (Act 2 Scene 1, line 33). Are these visions from his imagination, things he wishes to see? Or are they coming from his enchanters?

The witches prepared spells to show Macbeth four visions. He saw an armed head, a bloody child, a child with a tree in its hand and a show of eight kings in a row. They told him that he must fear Macduff, that no one born of woman shall harm him and that he would not be conquered until Birnam Wood came to Dunsinane. Macbeth gained confidence through this.

4:2

Lady Macduff, left by her husband in her castle, is visited by the Thane of Ross. Macduff did not tell her of his plan to leave. Ross implies that harm may come to her. Lady Macduff and her small son talk together about the boy's father. Ross leaves, a man rushes through with warning of danger.

1 *What had he done* what crime had he committed

3–4 *when our actions … traitors* flight will be seen as evidence of being a traitor

9–11 There are many references to birds in this scene.

MACBETH Came they not by you?

LENNOX   No, indeed, my lord.

MACBETH Infected be the air whereon they ride,
And damned all those that trust them. I did hear
The galloping of horses. Who was't came by?   140

LENNOX   'Tis two or three, my lord, that bring you word
Macduff is fled to England.

MACBETH   Fled to England?

LENNOX   Ay, my good lord.

MACBETH [*Aside*] Time, thou anticipat'st my dread exploits:
The flighty purpose never is o'ertook   145
Unless the deed go with it. From this moment
The very firstlings of my heart shall be
The firstlings of my hand. And even now,
To crown my thoughts with acts, be it thought and done:
The castle of Macduff I will surprise,   150
Seize upon Fife, give to th' edge o' the sword
His wife, his babes, and all unfortunate souls
That trace him in his line. No boasting like a fool;
This deed I'll do before this purpose cool.
But no more sights! [*Aloud*] Where are these gentlemen?
Come, bring me where they are.

                                                      [*Exeunt*

4:2   *Enter* LADY MACDUFF, *her* SON, *and* ROSS

LADY MACDUFF What had he done, to make him fly the land?

ROSS   You must have patience, madam.

LADY MACDUFF   .   He had none.
His flight was madness; when our actions do not,
Our fears do make us traitors.

ROSS   You know not
Whether it was his wisdom or his fear.   5

LADY MACDUFF Wisdom! To leave his wife, to leave his babes,
His mansion, and his titles in a place
From whence himself does fly? He loves us not:
He wants the natural touch; for the poor wren,
The most diminutive of birds, will fight,   10
Her young ones in her nest, against the owl.
All is the fear, and nothing is the love;
As little is the wisdom, where the flight
So runs against all reason.

15 *school* control

17 *fits o' th' season* referring to Macbeth's atrocities and moods in these times. *fits* may refer back to Lady Macbeth excusing Macbeth at the banquet (Act 3 Scene 4, line 54) 'the fit is momentary'.

19 *do not know ourselves* do not know each other, or are not aware of being traitors, or … ? Ross's speech here is confused and secretive.

24 –5 Things will stop being bad or get better, and be what they used to be. Ross is in a hurry and also dares not say anything clearly.

28–9 He would cry if he stayed longer (which would disgrace him as a man and embarrass her).

> *This is yet another setting and it is the only time we see Lady Macduff. How could an atmosphere of family life be created here?*
>
> *Ross is fumbling with his words and seems confused about what he is saying. Do you see him as a) a weak and nervous person; b) a bold person risking his life to warn her; or c) a spy for Macbeth?*

34–5 *lime … pitfall … gin* These are all ways to trap birds. Farmers put bird-lime on fields to ensnare birds. Their wings get stuck in it and they die. A pitfall is a ditch for trapping. A gin is a mechanical trap which grabs the bird's legs or wings. What is Lady Macduff's meaning?

36 *Poor … for* nobody wants to trap poor birds, like us, only rich ones

Ross   My dearest coz,
    I pray you school yourself. But, for your husband,   15
    He is noble, wise, judicious, and best knows
    The fits o' th' season. I dare not speak much further;
    But cruel are the times, when we are traitors
    And do not know ourselves; when we hold rumour
    From what we fear, yet know not what we fear,   20
    But float upon a wild and violent sea
    Each way, and move. I take my leave of you.
    Shall not be long but I'll be here again.
    Things at the worst will cease, or else climb upward
    To what they were before. My pretty cousin,   25
    Blessing upon you!

Lady Macduff   Fathered he is, and yet he's fatherless.

Ross   I am so much a fool, should I stay longer,
    It would be my disgrace and your discomfort.
    I take my leave at once.

                                          [*Exit*

Lady Macduff   Sirrah, your father's dead,   30
    And what will you do now? How will you live?

Son   As birds do, mother.

Lady Macduff   What, with worms and flies?

Son   With what I get, I mean; and so do they.

Lady Macduff   Poor bird, thou'dst never fear the net nor lime,
    The pitfall nor the gin.

Son   Why should I, mother?   35
    Poor birds they are not set for.
    My father is not dead, for all your saying.

Lady Macduff   Yes, he is dead. How wilt thou do for a father?

Son   Nay, how will you do for a husband?

Lady Macduff   Why, I can buy me twenty at any market.   40

Son   Then you'll buy 'em to sell again.

Lady Macduff   Thou speak'st with all thy wit, and yet i' faith
    With wit enough for thee.

Son   Was my father a traitor, mother?

Lady Macduff   Ay, that he was.   45

Son   What is a traitor?

Lady Macduff   Why, one that swears and lies.

Son   And be all traitors that do so?

Lady Macduff   Every one that does so is a traitor, and must be hanged.   50

Son   And must they all be hanged that swear and lie?

> *Lady Macduff is a contrast with Lady Macbeth in that she is a mother and she is seen in domestic harmony with her son. Would you play this scene to emphasise the contrast or could it be played to create pity for Lady Macbeth?*

Massacre of the Innocents.

56   *enow* enough

65   *Though … perfect* although I intend only the best for you

66   *doubt* fear

70   *fell* terrible

71   *nigh* near. Is he hinting that something terrible is very close?

75   *laudable* worthy of praise

82   The little son's loyalty to his father is touching.

Compare the way two women are represented – eg, Lady Macduff's terms of endearment for her son (lines 34, 58, 63) and Lady Macbeth's request for her milk to be turned to gall (Act 1 Scene 5, line 47).

Also compare this killing to the other two murders in the play (Act 2 Scene 2 and Act 3 Scene 3).

Ross warned Lady Macduff of danger. She and her son spoke about Macduff and then they were both murdered. The mother and son died bravely, cursing the murderers.

LADY MACDUFF   Every one.

SON   Who must hang them?

LADY MACDUFF   Why, the honest men.

SON   Then the liars and swearers are fools; for there are   55
liars and swearers enow to beat the honest men, and
hang up them.

LADY MACDUFF   Now God help thee, poor monkey. But
how wilt thou do for a father?

SON   If he were dead, you'd weep for him; if you would   60
not, it were a good sign that I should quickly have a
new father.

LADY MACDUFF   Poor prattler, how thou talk'st!

Enter a MESSENGER

MESSENGER   Bless you, fair dame! I am not to you known,
Though in your state of honour I am perfect.   65
I doubt some danger does approach you nearly.
If you will take a homely man's advice,
Be not found here; hence, with your little ones.
To fright you thus, methinks I am too savage;
To do worse to you were fell cruelty,   70
Which is too nigh your person. Heaven preserve you!
I dare abide no longer.   [*Exit*

LADY MACDUFF   Whither should I fly?
I have done no harm. But I remember now
I am in this earthly world, where to do harm
Is often laudable, to do good sometime   75
Accounted dangerous folly. Why then, alas,
Do I put up that womanly defence
To say I have done no harm?

Enter MURDERERS

                 What are these faces?

FIRST MURDERER Where is your husband?

LADY MACDUFF   I hope in no place so unsanctified   80
Where such as thou mayst find him.

FIRST MURDERER   He's a traitor.

SON   Thou liest, thou shag-haired villain,

FIRST MURDERER   What, you egg!   [*Stabs him*
Young fry of treachery!

SON   He has killed me, mother;
Run away, I pray you.   [*Dies*

Exit LADY MACDUFF, *crying 'Murder!' and pursued by the* MURDERERS

4:3

In England, Macduff visits Malcolm, who suspects he has been sent by Macbeth to trick him. He tests him before he trusts him. The holy king of England has a special skill which enables him to cure disease by his touch alone. Ross arrives from Scotland with news for Macduff.

3	*mortal* deadly
4	*birthdom* native land
6	*resounds* echoes
8	*like syllable of dolour* with a similar sound of pain
9	*redress* put right
10	*to friend* to find friends to help me
12	*whose sole name* whose name alone
14	*He hath not touched you yet* he has not hurt you yet. This is horribly ironic.
15	*deserve of him through me* be rewarded by Macbeth (for betraying Malcolm, possibly). *and wisdom* and it may be wise
19–20	*recoil / In an imperial charge* give in and turn to evil if commanded by a king. Malcolm is very suspicious of Macduff.
22	*the brightest* Lucifer, God's favourite angel, rebelled in heaven and was thrown down to hell. That is how Satan came to be in hell. The implication is that rebels are thereby associated with hell!
23–4	*Though … look so* although bad people want to look like good ones, good ones also must look good
23	*foul* another echo of 'foul is fair'
24	*hopes* an audience knows already that Macduff's family has been murdered, so the word is tragically ironic. Macduff means hopes of counting on Malcolm to lead a rebellion against Macbeth.
25	*doubts* Malcolm is suspicious that Macduff is in alliance with Macbeth because he left his family
26	*rawness* exposed condition
29	*jealousies* suspicions
33	*check* challenge
34	*affeered* fixed. He means Macbeth will keep the title of King.
37	*to boot* as well

Malcolm is friendly but suspicious. Would he shake hands and offer Macduff a drink or have him frisked and closely guarded? Are the two men alone or are there soldiers or servants or friends with them? Macduff could make a sudden movement and Malcolm's hand could fly to his weapon.

4:3   *Enter* MALCOLM *and* MACDUFF

MALCOLM   Let us seek out some desolate shade, and there
          Weep our sad bosoms empty.

MACDUFF   Let us rather
          Hold fast the mortal sword, and like good men
          Bestride our down-fall'n birthdom. Each new morn
          New widows howl, new orphans cry, new sorrows   5
          Strike heaven on the face, that it resounds
          As if it felt with Scotland and yelled out
          Like syllable of dolour.

MALCOLM   What I believe, I'll wail;
          What know, believe; and what I can redress,
          As I shall find the time to friend, I will.   10
          What you have spoke, it may be so perchance.
          This tyrant, whose sole name blisters our tongues,
          Was once thought honest; you have loved him well;
          He hath not touched you yet. I am young, but something
          You may deserve of him through me, and wisdom   15
          To offer up a weak, poor, innocent lamb
          T'appease an angry god.

MACDUFF   I am not treacherous.

MALCOLM   But Macbeth is.
          A good and virtuous nature may recoil
          In an imperial charge. But I shall crave your pardon: 20
          That which you are, my thoughts cannot transpose;
          Angels are bright still, though the brightest fell;
          Though all things foul would wear the brows of grace,
          Yet grace must still look so.

MACDUFF   I have lost my hopes.

MALCOLM   Perchance even there where I did find my doubts.   25
          Why in that rawness left you wife and child,
          Those precious motives, those strong knots of love,
          Without leave-taking? I pray you,
          Let not my jealousies be your dishonours,
          But mine own safeties: you may be rightly just,   30
          Whatever I shall think.

MACDUFF   Bleed, bleed, poor country!
          Great tyranny, lay thou thy basis sure,
          For goodness dare not check thee; wear thou thy wrongs,
          The title is affeered. Fare thee well, lord;
          I would not be the villain that thou think'st   35
          For the whole space that's in the tyrant's grasp,
          And the rich East to boot.

43   *England* the king of England, Edward the Confessor

48   *sundry* various

49   *By him that shall succeed* by myself when I take over the crown

50   From here on, Malcolm describes his vices. These, he says, would make him a terrible king.

52   *opened* like buds. An image of grafted plants. Does this link Malcolm with Banquo?

55   *confineless* boundless

58   *luxurious* lustful

59   *Sudden* hasty, passionate, violent

63   *cistern* tank or pool, often containing snakes. It could recall a cauldron.

64–5   *All continent … will* would beat down any idea of chastity that tries to stop my desire

66–7   *intemperance … In nature is a tyranny* lack of control can tyrannise over a person's character

70   *what is yours* the crown

71   *Convey* arrange. *pleasures* sexual enjoyment

72   *And yet seem cold* and still seem not over-sexed.
       time world. *hoodwink* cheat

75   *greatness* a king, in this context. (He says lots of women are happy to go to bed with a king! There is some debate about Macduff's attitude to women here.)

MALCOLM   Be not offended;
　　　I speak not as in absolute fear of you.
　　　I think our country sinks beneath the yoke;
　　　It weeps, it bleeds, and each new day a gash   **40**
　　　Is added to her wounds. I think, withal,
　　　There would be hands uplifted in my right;
　　　And here from gracious England have I offer
　　　Of goodly thousands. But, for all this,
　　　When I shall tread upon the tyrant's head   **45**
　　　Or wear it on my sword, yet my poor country
　　　Shall have more vices than it had before,
　　　More suffer, and more sundry ways than ever,
　　　By him that shall succeed.

MACDUFF   What should he be?

MALCOLM   It is myself I mean; in whom I know   **50**
　　　All the particulars of vice so grafted
　　　That, when they shall be opened, black Macbeth
　　　Will seem as pure as snow, and the poor state
　　　Esteem him as a lamb, being compared
　　　With my confineless harms.

MACDUFF   Not in the legions   **55**
　　　Of horrid hell can come a devil more damned
　　　In evils to top Macbeth.

MALCOLM   I grant him bloody,
　　　Luxurious, avaricious, false, deceitful,
　　　Sudden, malicious, smacking of every sin
　　　That has a name; but there's no bottom, none,   **60**
　　　In my voluptuousness: your wives, your daughters,
　　　Your matrons, and your maids, could not fill up
　　　The cistern of my lust; and my desire
　　　All continent impediments would o'erbear
　　　That did oppose my will. Better Macbeth,   **65**
　　　Than such a one to reign.

MACDUFF   Boundless intemperance
　　　In nature is a tyranny; it hath been
　　　The untimely emptying of the happy throne,
　　　And fall of many kings. But fear not yet
　　　To take upon you what is yours: you may   **70**
　　　Convey your pleasures in a spacious plenty,
　　　And yet seem cold – the time you may so hoodwink.
　　　We have willing dames enough; there cannot be
　　　That vulture in you to devour so many
　　　As will to greatness dedicate themselves,   **75**
　　　Finding it so inclined.

MALCOLM   With this there grows

77 *affection* character

78 *staunchless avarice* unstoppable greed

79 *cut off* kill

85 *Sticks deeper* hurts more. Remember Macbeth's 'fears in Banquo / Stick deep' (Act 3 Scene 1, lines 48–9).

87 *sword* death

88 *foisons* plenty

89 *mere own* your own possessions, property. *portable* acceptable

> This is an unrealistic scene. How is it possible to make the dialogue seem like a proper conversation between two sensible people? Malcolm's testing of Macduff is an excuse for this long conversation about the virtues and vices of kingship. Some productions cut it heavily. Some emphasise the mistrust by using a door or gate to separate characters.

92 *verity* truthfulness

93 *Bounty* generosity

95–6 *but abound … crime* but I love to commit all the little variations of each crime

99 *Uproar* make chaos out of. *confound* throw into confusion

100 *All unity on earth* Macbeth has destroyed unity or togetherness, as we saw at the banquet.

106 *truest issue* rightful inheritor

107 *interdiction* condemnation

108 *blaspheme* swear vehemently against

110 *Oftener … feet* more often praying than walking. Shakespeare makes Malcolm's parents very holy.

116 *Wiped the black scruples* taken away all my doubts and suspicions

In my most ill-composed affection such
A staunchless avarice that, were I King,
I should cut off the nobles for their lands,
Desire his jewels and this other's house;   **80**
And my more-having would be as a sauce
To make me hunger more, that I should forge
Quarrels unjust against the good and loyal,
Destroying them for wealth.

MACDUFF   This avarice
Sticks deeper, grows with more pernicious root   **85**
Than summer-seeming lust; and it hath been
The sword of our slain kings. Yet do not fear;
Scotland hath foisons to fill up your will
Of your mere own. All these are portable,
With other graces weighed.   **90**

MALCOLM   But I have none. The king-becoming graces.
As justice, verity, temperance, stableness,
Bounty, perseverance, mercy, lowliness,
Devotion, patience, courage, fortitude –
I have no relish of them, but abound   **95**
In the division of each several crime,
Acting it many ways. Nay, had I power, I should
Pour the sweet milk of concord into hell,
Uproar the universal peace, confound
All unity on earth.

MACDUFF   O Scotland, Scotland!   **100**

MALCOLM   If such a one be fit to govern, speak.
I am as I have spoken.

MACDUFF   Fit to govern!
No, not to live. O nation miserable!
With an untitled tyrant bloody-sceptered,
When shalt thou see they wholesome days again,   **105**
Since that the truest issue of thy throne
By his own interdiction stands accursed,
And does blaspheme his breed? Thy royal father
Was a most sainted King; the Queen that bore thee,
Oftener upon her knees than on her feet,   **110**
Died every day she lived. Fare thee well,
These evils thou repeat'st upon thyself
Hath banished me from Scotland. O my breast,
Thy hope ends here!

MALCOLM   Macduff, this noble passion,
Child of integrity, hath from my soul   **115**
Wiped the black scruples, reconciled my thoughts
To thy good truth and honour. Devilish Macbeth

118   *trains* leads (for example, to a keg of gunpowder) and plots (word used in hawking)

123   *Unspeak mine own detraction* take back the bad things I have said about myself

126   *Unknown to woman* a virgin. *was forsworn* broke an oath

127   *coveted* desired

128   *broke my faith* told a lie

136–7   *the chance … quarrel* may our chance of success be as good as the justice of our cause

> *How can you show the sudden change in attitude here? Does Malcolm throw his arms around Macduff, or dismiss his guard, or finally offer him something to eat or drink? This last might fit in well with the feasting metaphors in the play.*

141   *wretched souls* poor, miserable people

142   *stay his cure* wait for him to cure their illnesses

By many of these trains hath sought to win me
Into his power, and modest wisdom plucks me
From over-credulous haste. But God above   **120**
Deal between thee and me; for even now
I put myself to thy direction, and
Unspeak mine own detraction; here abjure
The taints and blames I laid upon myself,
For strangers to my nature. I am yet   **125**
Unknown to woman, never was forsworn,
Scarcely have coveted what was mine own,
At no time broke my faith, would not betray
The devil to his fellow, and delight
No less in truth than life – my first false speaking   **130**
Was this upon myself. What I am truly
Is thine and my poor country's to command;
Whither, indeed, before thy here-approach,
Old Siward, with ten thousand warlike men
Already at a point, was setting forth.   **135**
Now we'll together, and the chance of goodness
Be like our warranted quarrel. Why are you silent?

MACDUFF   Such welcome and unwelcome things at once
'Tis hard to reconcile.

Enter a DOCTOR

MALCOLM   Well, more anon.
Comes the King forth, I pray you?   **140**

DOCTOR   Ay, sir; there are a crew of wretched souls
That stay his cure. Their malady convinces
The great assay of art; but at his touch,
Such sanctity hath heaven given his hand,
They presently amend.

MALCOLM   I thank you, doctor.   [*Exit* DOCTOR **145**

MACDUFF   What's the disease he means?

MALCOLM   'Tis called the Evil –
A most miraculous work in this good King,
Which often since my here-remain in England
I have seen him do. How he solicits heaven
Himself best knows; but strangely-visited people,   **150**
All swoln and ulcerous, pitiful to the eye,
The mere despair of surgery, he cures,
Hanging a golden stamp about their necks,
Put on with holy prayers; and 'tis spoken,
To the succeeding royalty he leaves   **155**
The healing benediction. With this strange virtue
He hath a heavenly gift of prophecy,
And sundry blessings hang about his throne

S.D. *Enter Ross* It is ironic that Ross comes a second time to bring news of a treacherous Thane of Cawdor. When was the first time?

166–7 *where nothing … to smile.* people can only happily survive if they pretend to know nothing

168 *rend* tear

169 *not marked* either: but not noticed – implying that among so many shrieks, one more is not noticed; or: but not mentioned – implying that nobody dare say anything

170 *a modern ecstasy* just a common madness. *knell* funeral bell

173 *or ere* before

173–4 *O relation / Too nice* what a story, too full of detail

175–6 *That of an hour … new one* when the latest catastrophe is only an hour old, it is already overtaken by a new one, so that the person giving the account is hissed at as bringing old news

176 *teems* gives birth to

Ross is given a most eloquent and poetic speech vividly describing the pain of living in a country crippled by violence and suspicion. In a film version a camera could show some of these horrors. What would you choose to show in a film?

The responses of the two listeners are short and could show impatience, agreement, or other reaction.

180 *a niggard* a mean person

182 *Which I have heavily borne* which was a burden for me. Is he suggesting bad news for Macduff?

183 *out* rebelling

185 *For that … a-foot* because I saw Macbeth's army mobilised

186 *your eye* your presence. He speaks to Malcolm here.

188 *doff … dire … distresses* shake off their miserable troubles. Notice the strong alliteration. What is its effect?

That speak him full of grace.

Enter **Ross**

MACDUFF   See who comes here.

MALCOLM   My countryman; but yet I know him not.   **160**

MACDUFF   My ever-gentle cousin, welcome hither.

MALCOLM   I know him now. Good God, betimes remove
The means that makes us strangers!

ROSS   Sir, amen.

MACDUFF   Stands Scotland where it did?

ROSS   Alas, poor country,
Almost afraid to know itself. It cannot   **165**
Be called our mother, but our grave: where nothing
But who knows nothing, is once seen to smile;
Where sighs and groans and shrieks that rend the air
Are made, not marked; where violent sorrow seems
A modern ecstasy. The dead man's knell   **170**
Is there scarce asked for who, and good men's lives
Expire before the flowers in their caps,
Dying or ere they sicken.

MACDUFF   O relation
Too nice, and yet too true!

MALCOLM   What's the newest grief?

ROSS   That of an hour's age doth hiss the speaker;   **175**
Each minute teems a new one.

MACDUFF   How does my wife?

ROSS   Why, well.

MACDUFF   And all my children?

ROSS   Well too.

MACDUFF   The tyrant has not battered at their peace?

ROSS   No; they were well at peace when I did leave 'em.

MACDUFF   Be not a niggard of your speech. How goes't?   **180**

ROSS   When I came hither to transport the tidings,
Which I have heavily borne, there ran a rumour
Of many worthy fellows that were out;
Which was to my belief witnessed the rather
For that I saw the tyrant's power a-foot.   **185**
Now is the time of help; your eye in Scotland
Would create soldiers, make our women fight
To doff their dire distresses.

MALCOLM   Be't their comfort
We are coming thither. Gracious England hath
Lent us good Siward and ten thousand men –   **190**

195 *latch* catch

196 *fee-grief* sorrow for an individual

205 *To relate the manner* if I told you how they were killed

206 *quarry* animals killed in hunting. *deer* the animal and 'dear ones'

216 *He has no children* This is much quoted to prove that Macbeth has no children. It could mean Malcolm. What do you think Macduff means by this?

218 *dam* mother. Birds are used again in this scene to describe Macduff's family.

An older and a better soldier none
That Christendom gives out.

Ross   Would I could answer
This comfort with the like. But I have words
That would be howled out in the desert air,
Where hearing should not latch them.

Macduff   What concern they?   **195**
The general cause; or is it a fee-grief
Due to some single breast?

Ross   No mind that's honest
But in it shares some woe, though the main part
Pertains to you alone.

Macduff   If it be mine,
Keep it not from me; quickly let me have it.   **200**

Ross   Let not your ears despise my tongue for ever,
Which shall possess them with the heaviest sound
That ever yet they heard.

Macduff   Humh! I guess at it.

Ross   Your castle is surprised; your wife and babes
Savagely slaughtered. To relate the manner   **205**
Were, on the quarry of these murdered deer,
To add the death of you.

Malcolm   Merciful heaven!
What, man, ne'er pull your hat upon your brows;
Give sorrow words. The grief that does not speak
Whispers the o'er-fraught heart and bids it break.   **210**

Macduff   My children too?

Ross   Wife, children, servants, all
That could be found.

Macduff   And I must be from thence!
My wife killed too?

Ross   I have said.

Malcolm   Be comforted;
Let's make us medicines of our great revenge
To cure this deadly grief.   **215**

Macduff   He has no children. – All my pretty ones?
Did you say all? – O hell-kite! – All?
What, all my pretty chickens and their dam
At one fell swoop?

Malcolm   Dispute it like a man.

Macduff   I shall do so;   **220**
But I must also feel it as a man.
I cannot but remember such things were

226   *demerits* faults

> *Does Macduff suspect what Ross has to tell him? Why does Ross not tell him immediately?*
>
> *Does he show his pain when he hears the news? At first his lines are short questions, then his feelings loosen and words tumble out.*
>
> *How would Malcolm and Ross react? Remember that Malcolm had implied that Macduff had taken a dangerous risk leaving his family unprotected. Pauses can be used effectively in this scene of high emotion. Where would you choose to put pauses?*

228   *whetstone* stone for sharpening a knife or sword

228–9   *Let grief … enrage it* Malcolm is now the one telling Macduff to get angry. Their positions have changed from the beginning of the scene. Look back to the first lines.

232   *intermission* interruption

233   *fiend of Scotland* Macbeth of course. He is now seen as like a devil. Do not forget that these people know nothing of Macbeth's meeting with the witches.

240   *The night … day* it is a long night that does not have a day at the end of it (a positive statement of hope). The rhyming couplet gives it an air of decisive action and hope for a harmonious outcome.

> *How could you make a difference between Scotland and England? You could use ceremonial music, colours, accents. One production set this scene in a chapel. Would you give the place a character? It is only used for this one scene, but it is a long one of 240 lines.*

Compare this scene with the previous one in Macduff's castle. News is heard in both; important topics are discussed, such as tyranny, kingship; Ross is in both. How do the two scenes compare and to what effect?

Macduff visited Malcolm in England. Malcolm tested his loyalty and then trusted his good motives for coming. Ross arrived and told Macduff about the murder of his wife and children. They then decided to take an army against Macbeth with England's help.

That were most precious to me. Did heaven look on,
And would not take their part? Sinful Macduff,
They were all struck for thee. Naught that I am,   **225**
Not for their own demerits, but for mine,
Fell slaughter on their souls. Heaven rest them now.

MALCOLM   Be this the whetstone of your sword. Let grief
Convert to anger; blunt not the heart, enrage it.

MACDUFF   O, I could play the woman with mine eyes,   **230**
And braggart with my tongue. But gentle heavens,
Cut short all intermission. Front to front
Bring thou this fiend of Scotland and myself;
Within my sword's length set him; if he scape,
Heaven forgive him too!

MALCOLM   This tune goes manly.   **235**
Come, go we to the King. Our power is ready;
Our lack is nothing but our leave. Macbeth
Is ripe for shaking, and the powers above
Put on their instruments. Receive what cheer you may;
The night is long that never finds the day.   [*Exeunt* **240**

5:1

It is night-time. Macbeth is preparing to defend himself against the invasion from England. A doctor and Lady Macbeth's waiting woman have watched for two nights to see Lady Macbeth sleep-walking. They see the light of a candle and Lady Macbeth comes in.

9 *perturbation in nature* disorder in natural health

10 *do the effects of watching* act as if she were awake

14 *which I will not report* The waiting woman is nervous of committing herself.

16 *meet* right or fitting

19 *her very guise* her habitual behaviour

38–9 *call our power to account* no one can prove anything against a tyrant

40 *blood* The blood she imagines on her hands and possibly a reference to Duncan's son, his blood heir, who is invading Macbeth's right to the throne.

Enter Lady Macbeth with a taper.

116

5:1   *Enter a* DOCTOR OF PHYSIC *and a* WAITING GENTLEWOMAN

DOCTOR   I have two nights watched with you, but can
perceive no truth in your report. When was it she last
walked?

GENTLEWOMAN   Since his Majesty went into the field, I   5
have seen her rise from her bed, throw her nightgown
upon her, unlock her closet, take forth paper, fold it,
write upon't, read it, afterwards seal it, and again
return to bed; yet all this while in a most fast sleep.

DOCTOR   A great perturbation in nature, to receive at
once the benefit of sleep and do the effects of watching.   10
In this slumbery agitation, besides her walking and
other actual performances, what, at any time, have you
heard her say?

GENTLEWOMAN   That, sir, which I will not report after
her.   15

DOCTOR   You may to me, and 'tis most meet you should.

GENTLEWOMAN   Neither to you nor any one, having no
witness to confirm my speech.

Enter LADY MACBETH *with a taper*

Lo you, here she comes. This is her very guise; and
upon my life, fast asleep. Observe her; stand close.   20

DOCTOR   How came she by that light?

GENTLEWOMAN   Why, it stood by her; she has light by
her continually, 'tis her command.

DOCTOR   You see her eyes are open.

GENTLEWOMAN   Ay, but their sense is shut.   25

DOCTOR   What is it she does now? Look, how she rubs
her hands.

GENTLEWOMAN   It is an accustomed action with her, to
seem thus washing her hands. I have known her continue
in this a quarter of an hour.   30

LADY MACBETH   Yet here's a spot.

DOCTOR   Hark! she speaks. I will set down what comes
from her, to satisfy my remembrance the more
strongly.

LADY MACBETH   Out, damned spot! Out, I say! – One;   35
two; why, then 'tis time to do't. – Hell is murky. – Fie,
my lord, fie! A soldier, and afeard? What need we
fear who knows it, when none can call our power to
account? Yet who would have thought the old man to
have had so much blood in him?   40

117

> *We have not seen Lady Macbeth since Act 3 Scene 4, line 143. Has she changed in appearance, movement, voice? Does she now evoke pity or horror or both, or some other reaction?*
>
> *What is the paper? Could it be the letter from Macbeth in Act 1 Scene 5 or her diary?*
>
> *Do the doctor and waiting woman whisper? Do they move about? Lady Macbeth's reaction, or non-reaction, to them will prove to an audience that she is sleep-walking.*

44–5   *you mar all with this starting* you spoil everything with your fits and nervousness

53–4   *sorely charged* heavily weighed down

58   *Pray God it be, sir.* The waiting woman hopes all will be well.

64   *on's grave* of his grave

67   *Come … come* Repetitions were seen as a sign of mental distress.

68   *done … undone* This echoes Act 1 Scene 6 line 15, Act 1 Scene 7 line 1 and Act 3 Scene 2 line 12 – to what effect?

72   *Foul whisperings are abroad* dreadful rumours are around

74   *discharge* give out. It sounds like an infection.

75   *a divine* a priest

79   *mated* overcome. The scene ends with a rhyming couplet.

> *Would you have some real water on the stage? This is a very quiet scene and the noise of splashing can be effective. Should the scene be played with some visible props – for example, a mirror, a dressing table with perfumes on it – or should there be nothing there at all?*

Compare this scene with another middle-of-the-night scene, in which Macbeth hallucinates and sees a dagger (Act 2 Scene 1, line 33). Are there any similarities?

Compare it with that same night scene directly after the murder of Duncan, when Macbeth says he has murdered sleep (Act 2 Scene 2).

Compare it also with Lady Macbeth's last appearance before this scene (Act 3 Scene 4).

Lady Macbeth walked and talked in her sleep. The doctor and waiting woman heard her speaking of blood on her hand and of murders she seemed to know about.

DOCTOR   Do you mark that?

LADY MACBETH   The Thane of Fife had a wife; where is
        she now? – What, will these hands ne'er be clean? –
        No more o' that, my lord, no more o' that; you mar
        all with this starting.   45

DOCTOR   Go to, go to; you have known what you should
        not.

GENTLEWOMAN   She has spoke what she should not, I
        am sure of that; Heaven knows what she has known.

LADY MACBETH   Here's the smell of the blood still: all   50
        the perfumes of Arabia will not sweeten this little
        hand. Oh, oh, oh!

DOCTOR   What a sigh is there! The heart is sorely
        charged.

GENTLEWOMAN   I would not have such a heart in my   55
        bosom for the dignity of the whole body.

DOCTOR   Well, well, well.

GENTLEWOMAN   Pray God it be, sir.

DOCTOR   This disease is beyond my practice. Yet I have
        known those which have walked in their sleep who   60
        have died holily in their beds.

LADY MACBETH   Wash your hands, put on your nightgown;
        look not so pale. – I tell you yet again, Banquo's
        buried; he cannot come out on's grave.

DOCTOR   Even so?   65

LADY MACBETH   To bed, to bed; there's knocking at the
        gate. Come, come, come, come, give me your hand.
        What's done cannot be undone. To bed, to bed, to
        bed.   [*Exit*

DOCTOR   Will she go now to bed?   70

GENTLEWOMAN   Directly.

DOCTOR   Foul whisperings are abroad. Unnatural deeds
        Do breed unnatural troubles; infected minds
        To their deaf pillows will discharge their secrets.
        More needs she the divine than the physician.   75
        God, God forgive us all! Look after her;
        Remove from her the means of all annoyance,
        And still keep eyes upon her. So, good night.
        My mind she has mated, and amazed my sight;
        I think, but dare not speak.

GENTLEWOMAN   Good night, good doctor.   80

                                              [*Exeunt*

119

5:2

The rebel thanes within Scotland wait to join with the invading forces from England led by Malcolm and Macduff. One tells how Macbeth has walled himself into the castle of Dunsinane, where his forces defend him.

2	*uncle Siward* Malcolm's grandfather on his mother's side. 'Uncle' is used for an older male relative.
3	*dear causes* motivations for war, which are very close to their hearts
4	*bleeding* the bloody battlefield and/or taking of blood, which was done to cure a fever
5	*Excite the mortified man* rouse the man who has been offended or a man who is almost dead. *Birnam* again, an echo from the witches
8–9	*file / Of all the gentry* list of all the men of rank
10	*unrough* not old enough to have beards
15–16	*He cannot buckle ... belt of rule.* he cannot control his passions beneath his belt and/or country beneath his rule
19–20	*only in command / Nothing in love* only because they are forced to, not because they love the king
21	*giant's robe* Another clothing image.
22–5	*Who then ... being there* Macbeth's senses are in rebellion against his acts.
26	*where 'tis truly owed* to Malcolm, the rightful heir
27	*medicine ... sickly* disease and cure imagery again. *weal* country
28	*purge* cleansing. Their blood will act as a cleaning of Scotland's illness.
30	*sovereign flower* flower of true kingship and/or the healthy flower that will be medicine for the kingdom (another metaphor about healthy growth). Rhyming couplet.

*There are many words in this scene which recall other scenes: **shall we well meet them, murders sticking on his hands, hang loose about him, the sovereign flower**, and so on. In production how could you unostentatiously show these echoes visually? For example, when Lady Macbeth says **the innocent flower** in Act 1 Scene 5, line 64, she could pick one and a soldier could do the same here. The witches' words are also used.*

Compare the words used about Macbeth in this scene, **dwarfish**, **tyrant**, with those used of him in Act 1 Scene 2.

This army is marching in organised control. Compare it to Macbeth's army in the next scene.

The rebel thanes told of how Macbeth's forces remain with him not by choice and of how some revolted. Their army moved towards Birnam wood.

5:2

Enter, with drum and colours, MENTEITH, CAITHNESS,
ANGUS, LENNOX, *and* SOLDIERS

MENTEITH The English power is near, led on by Malcolm,
    His uncle Siward, and the good Macduff.
    Revenges burn in them; for their dear causes
    Would to the bleeding and the grim alarm
    Excite the mortified man.

ANGUS   Near Birnam wood   **5**
    Shall we well meet them; that way are they coming.

CAITHNESS Who knows if Donalbain be with his brother?

LENNOX   For certain, sir, he is not. I have a file
    Of all the gentry; there is Siward's son,
    And many unrough youths that even now   **10**
    Protest their first of manhood.

MENTEITH   What does the tyrant?

CAITHNESS Great Dunsinane he strongly fortifies.
    Some say he's mad; others, that lesser hate him,
    Do call it valiant fury; but, for certain,
    He cannot buckle his distempered cause   **15**
    Within the belt of rule.

ANGUS   Now does he feel
    His secret murders sticking on his hands;
    Now minutely revolts upbraid his faith-breach;
    Those he commands move only in command,
    Nothing in love. Now does he feel his title   **20**
    Hang loose about him, like a giant's robe
    Upon a dwarfish thief.

MENTEITH   Who then shall blame
    His pestered senses to recoil and start,
    When all that is within him does condemn
    Itself for being there?

CAITHNESS   Well, march we on   **25**
    To give obedience where 'tis truly owed.
    Meet we the medicine of the sickly weal,
    And with him pour we, in our country's purge,
    Each drop of us.

LENNOX   Or so much as it needs
    To dew the sovereign flower and drown the weeds.   **30**
    Make we our march towards Birnam.

[Exeunt, marching

Macbeth has fortified his castle, Dunsinane, which is nearer to the English border than Forres, Duncan's castle. He comforts himself with the witches' prophecies that he would not be harmed. A servant tells him of the invading English forces. Lady Macbeth is incurably sick.

1 *let them fly all* the followers who have defected to Malcolm's camp

3 *taint* weaken

4 *spirits* figures he saw in the visions, which prophesied to him

8 *epicures* people who indulge themselves in fancy living

9 *sway by* rule myself by

12 *goose look* This image evokes white goose feathers and goose flesh, prickly with fear.

15 *lily-livered* a white liver meant no courage, as the liver was the seat of passion

16 *linen* linen cloth is also creamy white

17 *whey* skimmed milk, ie weak and watery-white

19 *Seyton* The Seyton family were long-standing armour bearers for the kings of Scotland.

20 *push* effort; or it could also mean attack from the invaders

21 *cheer* cheer me up; or perhaps a play on the word 'chair'.
   disseat Remember Banquo pushed him from his stool (or throne).

23 *sere* yellowed, withered, autumnal state

27 *mouth-honour* respect only given in words, not meant

We have not seen Macbeth since Act 4 Scene 1, when he heard his prophecies. Since then we have learned of the atrocities that he has committed, that his wife is incurably mad, that Malcolm and Macduff, strongly motivated, have joined forces with a thousand men to invade his castle. Has he changed in appearance, pace of words or actions, voice? (Notice, for example, his commanding, doubting, and complaining.) What actions could accompany the insults to the **cream-faced loon**?

5:3   *Enter* MACBETH, DOCTOR, *and* ATTENDANTS

MACBETH   Bring me no more reports; let them fly all.
          Till Birnam wood remove to Dunsinane,
          I cannot taint with fear. What's the boy Malcolm?
          Was he not born of woman? The spirits that know
          All mortal consequences have pronounced me thus: 5
          'Fear not, Macbeth; no man that's born of woman
          Shall e'er have power upon thee'. Then fly, false thanes,
          And mingle with the English epicures.
          The mind I sway by and the heart I bear
          Shall never sag with doubt nor shake with fear.   10

                    Enter a SERVANT
          The devil damn thee black, thou cream-faced loon!
          Where gott'st thou that goose look?

SERVANT   There is ten thousand –

MACBETH   Geese, villain?

SERVANT   Soldiers, sir.

MACBETH   Go prick thy face, and over-red thy fear,
          Thou lily-livered boy. What soldiers, patch?   15
          Death of thy soul! those linen cheeks of thine
          Are counsellors to fear. What soldiers, whey-face?

SERVANT   The English force, so please you.

MACBETH   Take thy face hence.   [*Exit* SERVANT
                    Seyton! – I am sick at heart
          When I behold – Seyton, I say! – This push   20
          Will cheer me ever, or disseat me now.
          I have lived long enough: my way of life
          Is fall'n into the sere, the yellow leaf;
          And that which should accompany old age,
          As honour, love, obedience, troops of friends,   25
          I must not look to have; but, in their stead,
          Curses, not loud but deep, mouth-honour, breath,
          Which the poor heart would fain deny, and dare not.
          Seyton!

                    Enter SEYTON

SEYTON   What's your gracious pleasure?

MACBETH   What news more?   30

SEYTON   All is confirmed, my lord, which was reported.

MACBETH   I'll fight, till from my bones my flesh be hacked.
          Give me my armour.

SEYTON   'Tis not needed yet.

MACBETH   I'll put it on.

35	*skirr* scour
42	*Raze* erase; literally scrape with a razor
43	*oblivious* making someone forget or be unaware of
47	*physic* doctor's medicine
50	*dispatch* hurry up
50–1	*cast / The water* examine the urine for diseases
52	*pristine* pure, as it was before infection
56	*rhubarb, senna* laxatives to empty the sytem of illness
58	*royal preparation* the forces collected and fortifications made
58	*Bring it after me* spoken to Seyton about the armour
59	*bane* poison
59–62	Rhyming couplets.

How does Seyton come in – rushing in fear, casual and calm, vindictively enjoying Macbeth's panic? He took a lot of calling. Here is another chance for a striking character part.

There is a doctor in the English court also. Would you contrast them obviously or make them similar?

Macbeth is almost touching here. If he had not been so murderous, he could be pitied. He swings in mood from violence – **hang those ... fear** – to melancholy meditation – **sweet oblivious antidote**. How could this be shown?

Is Macbeth's mind diseased in this scene? Compare his state of mind here with that of Lady Macbeth in Act 5 Scene 1.

Macbeth, full of false confidence, armed himself for battle.

5:4

The English army has met up with the Scottish rebels under Malcolm.

1	*Cousins* an immediate contrast with Macbeth's lack of family and friends

Send out moe horses, skirr the country round;   35
Hang those that talk of fear. Give me mine armour. –
How does your patient, doctor?

DOCTOR   Not so sick, my lord,
As she is troubled with thick-coming fancies
That keep her from her rest.

MACBETH   Cure her of that:
Canst thou not minister to a mind diseased,   40
Pluck from the memory a rooted sorrow,
Raze out the written troubles of the brain,
And with some sweet oblivious antidote
Cleanse the stuffed bosom of that perilous stuff
Which weighs upon the heart?

DOCTOR   Therein the patient   45
Must minister to himself.

MACBETH   Throw physic to the dogs, I'll none of it. –
Come, put mine armour on; give me my staff.
Seyton, send out. – Doctor, the thanes fly from me. –
Come, sir, dispatch. If thou couldst, doctor, cast   50
The water of my land, find her disease,
And purge it to a sound and pristine health,
I would applaud thee to the very echo,
That should applaud again. – Pull't off, I say. –   55
What rhubarb, senna, or what purgative drug
Would scour these English hence? Hear'st thou of them?

DOCTOR   Ay, my good lord; your royal preparation
Makes us hear something.

MACBETH   Bring it after me. –
I will not be afraid of death and bane
Till Birnam forest come to Dunsinane.   60

[*Exeunt all but* DOCTOR

DOCTOR   Were I from Dunsinane away and clear,
Profit again should hardly draw me here.

[*Exit

5:4   *Enter, with drum and colours,* MALCOLM, SIWARD, MACDUFF,
YOUNG SIWARD, MENTEITH, CAITHNESS, ANGUS, LENNOX, ROSS,
and SOLDIERS, *marching*

MALCOLM   Cousins, I hope the days are near at hand
That chambers will be safe.

MENTEITH   We doubt it nothing.

SIWARD   What wood is this before us?

MENTEITH   The wood of Birnam.

4   *hew* cut

5   *bear't before him* carry it in front of him

7   *Err in report of us* report our numbers mistakenly to the enemy

9   *Keeps* stays

10   *setting down* laying siege

11   *advantage to be gone* benefit to be gained from escaping

12   *more and less* people in positions of high rank and ordinary subjects

13   *constrainéd things* people forced to stay

19   *Thoughts … relate* thinking is only guesswork and uncertain

20   *But … arbitrate* only fighting gives certain results. This is similar to Macbeth's thoughts in Act 4 Scene 1, line 149. Two rhyming couplets.

The awful truth about Birnam wood is made clear here. This could be quite a long scene, even though there are not many words. To build up the suspense it could have soldiers chopping trees, the sounds of people shouting and branches crashing down. A tree could be shown falling across a stage. Felling a tree could be a symbol of killing a king, or possibly a family tree.

Now it is the rebels' turn for deception. They use it to advantage. Compare this simple military deception with the deception of the witches and their spirits in Act 4 Scene 1.

Malcolm's army chopped down branches from Birnam wood to conceal their numbers from the enemy.

5:5

Macbeth in the castle hears news of the enemy coming nearer. He has a few followers left, who give him reports.

4   *ague* fever

5   *forced* reinforced

6   *dareful* boldly

11   *fell* mane, like an animal's hair. Remember when his hair did stand on end?

12   *treatise* story

13   *supped* imagery of eating again

14   *Direness* horror.

15   *start me* alarm me or make me jump

MALCOLM   Let every soldier hew him down a bough
          And bear't before him; thereby shall we shadow   5
          The numbers of our host, and make discovery
          Err in report of us.

SOLDIERS   It shall be done.

SIWARD   We learn no other but the confident tyrant
          Keeps still in Dunsinane,and will endure
          Our setting down before 't.

MALCOLM   'Tis his main hope,   10
          For where there is advantage to be gone
          Both more and less have given him the revolt,
          And none serve with him but constrainéd things
          Whose hearts are absent too.

MACDUFF   Let our just censures
          Attend the true event, and put we on   15
          Industrious soldiership.

SIWARD   The time approaches
          That will with due decision make us know
          What we shall say we have, and what we owe.
          Thoughts speculative their unsure hopes relate,
          But certain issue strokes must arbitrate;   20
          Towards which advance the war.

                                   [*Exeunt, marching*

5:5   *Enter, with drum and colours,* MACBETH, SEYTON, *and* SOLDIERS

MACBETH   Hang out our banners on the outward walls;
          The cry is still 'They come'. Our castle's strength
          Will laugh a siege to scorn. Here let them lie
          Till famine and the ague eat them up.
          Were they not forced with those that should be ours,   5
          We might have met them dareful, beard to beard,
          And beat them backward home.

                                   [*A cry of women within*
                    What is that noise?

SEYTON   It is the cry of women, my good lord.   [*Exit*

MACBETH   I have almost forgotten the taste of fears.
          The time has been my senses would have cooled   10
          To hear a night-shriek, and my fell of hair
          Would at a dismal treatise rouse and stir
          As life were in't. I have supped full with horrors;
          Direness, familiar to my slaughterous thoughts,
          Cannot once start me.

17 *hereafter* after the battle, or at some time in the future

23 *dusty death* reminiscent of 'ashes to ashes, dust to dust', part of the Christian funeral service

25 *struts and frets* a comment on acting. Actors sometimes march about and show passion.

28 A half line. What effect does this have?

The cry of women comes from Lady Macbeth's waiting women. What sort of cry would be best here? It could recall the witches' voices to make a link. Is it a sudden cry of horrified surprise or a funeral-type wail or hysterical screaming?

Macbeth says his senses are deadened. How would he react to the cry?

In the 'Tomorrow' speech, how could you use lighting effectively?

35 *The wood began to move* An example of dramatic irony.

40 *cling* shrink or shrivel, a witch-like curse

41 *if thou dost for me as much* if you do the same to me

42 *pull in resolution* draw in the final conclusion of events

43 *equivocation* double meanings

47 *avouches* affirms

51 *alarum bell* a reminder of the alarum bell that was rung when Duncan's body was discovered (Act 2 Scene 3, line 73). *wrack* ruin

52 *harness* his armour. Rhyming couplet.

The scene is full of conflicting moods. He is meditating, violent in speech, resigned. The calm, organised community of the attacking forces contrasts with the chaotic, friendless despair of Macbeth. Would you, in production, want to create sympathy for Macbeth or for the invaders? Is it possible to do both?

Compare the despair and feeling of pointlessness expressed in this scene, with the obsessive need for action and self-protection expressed by Macbeth in Act 3 Scene 1, lines 47–71. What do the two speeches show about his feelings about himself and others?

Macbeth heard women's cries and learned of his wife's death. He fell into deep despair. He was then told of the wood approaching Dunsinane.

Enter SEYTON

Wherefore was that cry?   15

SEYTON   The Queen, my lord, is dead.

MACBETH   She should have died hereafter;
There would have been a time for such a word.
Tomorrow, and tomorrow, and tomorrow,
Creeps in this petty pace from day to day,   20
To the last syllable of recorded time;
And all our yesterdays have lighted fools
The way to dusty death. Out, out, brief candle!
Life's but a walking shadow, a poor player
That struts and frets his hour upon the stage   25
And then is heard no more. It is a tale
Told by an idiot, full of sound and fury,
Signifying nothing.

Enter a MESSENGER

Thou comest to use thy tongue; thy story quickly.

MESSENGER Gracious my lord,   30
I should report that which I say I saw,
But know not how to do't.

MACBETH   Well, say, sir.

MESSENGER As I did stand my watch upon the hill,
I looked toward Birnam, and anon methought
The wood began to move.

MACBETH   Liar and slave!   35

MESSENGER Let me endure your wrath if't be not so.
Within this three mile may you see it coming;
I say, a moving grove.

MACBETH   If thou speak'st false,
Upon the next tree shalt thou hang alive
Till famine cling thee. If thy speech be sooth,   40
I care not if thou dost for me as much.
I pull in resolution, and begin
To doubt th'equivocation of the fiend,
That lies like truth: 'Fear not, till Birnam wood
Do come to Dunsinane'; and now a wood   45
Comes toward Dunsinane. Arm, arm, and out!
If this which he avouches does appear,
There is nor flying hence, nor tarrying here.
I 'gin to be aweary of the sun
And wish th' estate o' the world were now undone.   50
Ring the alarum bell! Blow wind, come wrack!
At least we'll die with harness on our back.

[*Exeunt*

5:6

Malcolm's army enters carrying branches. They throw them down, now they have arrived at the castle, and reveal their numbers. Siward and his teenage son are to lead the first battle.

4 *we* Malcolm could be using the royal plural already.

10 *harbingers* heralds

This is the last scene where we see the armies separately. How could you overcome the difficulty of having two groups of people, both armies, shown in different areas with little interval between them? This is easy enough to achieve in a film but on stage it is more complicated. Could there be only voices for some of the scenes, with Malcolm's army getting nearer?

5:7

The two armies meet. Macbeth encounters Siward's son first and kills him. Then Macduff hears what he thinks is the sounds of Macbeth fighting and challenges him. Malcolm and Siward enter the surrendered castle.

2 *bear* In the 16th century, bear-baiting took place near the theatre. The bear was tied to a post and dogs would snap at and bite it to make it angry.

5:6

Enter, with drum and colours, **Malcolm, Siward,**
Macduff, *and their Army, with boughs*

Malcolm   Now near enough; your leafy screens throw down,
And show like those you are. You, worthy uncle,
Shall with my cousin, your right noble son,
Lead our first battle. Worthy Macduff and we
Shall take upon's what else remains to do,   5
According to our order.

Siward   Fare you well.
Do we but find the tyrant's power tonight,
Let us be beaten, if we cannot fight.

Macduff   Make all our trumpets speak; give them all breath,
Those clamorous harbingers of blood and death.   10

[*Exeunt. Alarums*

5:7

Alarums. Enter **Macbeth**

Macbeth   They have tied me to a stake; I cannot fly,
But bear-like I must fight the course. What's he
That was not born of woman? Such a one
Am I to fear, or none.

Enter **Young Siward**

Young Siward What is thy name?

Macbeth   Thou'lt be afraid to hear it.   5

Young Siward No; though thou call'st thyself a hotter name
Than any is in hell.

Macbeth   My name's Macbeth.

Young Siward The devil himself could not pronounce a title
More hateful to mine ear.

Macbeth   No, nor more fearful.

Young Siward Thou liest, abhorred tyrant; with my sword   10
I'll prove the lie thou speak'st.

[*They fight, and* **Young Siward** *is slain.*

Macbeth   Thou wast born of woman.
But swords I smile at, weapons laugh to scorn,
Brandished by man that's of a woman born.

[*Exit*

Alarums. Enter **Macduff**

Macduff   That way the noise is. Tyrant, show thy face.
If thou be'st slain, and with no stroke of mine,   15
My wife and children's ghosts will haunt me still.

17 *kerns* hired soldiers, employed also in the battle in Act 1. Macduff implies that Macbeth has no loyal followers.

18 *staves* sticks, ie not sophisticated armour

20 *undeeded* without action or unused. Shakespeare made this word up. Does it apply to Macduff himself or to the sword?

21–2 *By this great clatter … Seems bruited* This great noise suggests the arrival of someone of importance. *fortune* fate

24 *gently rendered* surrendered without resistance

27 *The day … yours* success in the battle is nearly won

Noise and silence, movement and stillness can be used effectively in this scene.

A production could show dramatically how soldiers are changing sides in the middle of the fighting.

Compare the death of Siward's son in Act 5 Scene 7 with the death of Macduff's son in Act 4 Scene 2. Their deaths have different purposes and feelings.

5:8

Macduff, whose sword has been waiting for one man only, finally meets Macbeth on the battlefield. Macbeth refuses to give in to him and fights to the bitter end.

1 *the Roman fool* Roman soldiers would rather kill themselves than surrender.

5 *charged* weighed down

8 *Than terms can give thee out* than can be expressed in words

13 *Despair* do not trust in

14 *angel* bad angel, ie Lucifer, who used to be an angel in heaven before he was thrown into hell

16 *Untimely ripped* pulled from the womb before his time. This means he was born by Caesarian birth. This is a short line. It could leave space for Macbeth's astonishment.

I cannot strike at wretched kerns, whose arms
Are hired to bear their staves; either thou, Macbeth,
Or else my sword with an unbattered edge
I sheath again undeeded. There thou shouldst be;   20
By this great clatter, one of the greatest note
Seems bruited. Let me find him, fortune.
And more I beg not.   [*Exit. Alarums*

Enter MALCOLM *and* SIWARD

SIWARD   This way, my lord; the castle's gently rendered.
The tyrant's people on both sides do fight;   25
The noble thanes do bravely in the war;
The day almost itself professes yours,
And little is to do.

MALCOLM   We have met with foes
That strike beside us.

SIWARD   Enter, sir, the castle.   [*Exeunt. Alarum*

5:8   *Enter* MACBETH

MACBETH   Why should I play the Roman fool, and die
On my own sword? Whiles I see lives, the gashes
Do better upon them.

Enter MACDUFF

MACDUFF   Turn, hell-hound, turn!

MACBETH   Of all men else I have avoided thee.
But get thee back, my soul is too much charged   5
With blood of thine already.

MACDUFF   I have no words;
My voice is in my sword, thou bloodier villain
Than terms can give thee out!   [*They fight*

MACBETH   Thou losest labour;
As easy mayst thou the intrenchant air
With thy keen sword impress as make me bleed.   10
Let fall thy blade on vulnerable crests;
I bear a charmèd life, which must not yield
To one of woman born.

MACDUFF   Despair thy charm;
And let the angel whom thou still hast served
Tell thee, Macduff was from his mother's womb   15
Untimely ripped.

18 *cowed my better part of man* turned my courage to cowardice

19 *juggling fiends* equivocating witches and their spirits

20 *palter* haggle like a market woman

29 *baited* again like a bear

34 *damned* nearly Macbeth's last word

> There are two extremes of emotion here. Macduff is confident and Macbeth is shocked and shaken. When he discovers how he has misinterpreted the witches' prophecy, there could be accompanying sound or some shadow that goes away as a light comes on. Is it best to have Macbeth beheaded on stage or off?

5:9

The allies against Macbeth, having won the day, count their losses and proclaim Malcolm King of Scotland.

3 *cheaply bought* with very few lives lost

5 *paid a soldier's debt* been killed. It is a compliment to such a young man to call him a soldier.

8 *unshrinking station* position of military courage from which he did not shrink

12 *before* on the front of his body

MACBETH   Accurséd be that tongue that tells me so,
          For it hath cowed my better part of man.
          And be these juggling fiends no more believed,
          That palter with us in a double sense;   20
          That keep the word of promise to our ear,
          And break it to our hope. I'll not fight with thee.

MACDUFF   Then yield thee, coward,
          And live to be the show and gaze o' th' time.
          We'll have thee, as our rarer monsters are,   25
          Painted upon a pole, and underwrit,
          'Here may you see the tyrant'.

MACBETH   I will not yield
          To kiss the ground before young Malcolm's feet,
          And to be baited with the rabble's curse.
          Though Birnam wood be come to Dunsinane,   30
          And thou opposed, being of no woman born,
          Yet I will try the last. Before my body
          I throw my warlike shield: lay on, Macduff,
          And damned be him that first cries 'Hold, enough!'

                                                    [*Exeunt fighting*

            Alarums. Re-enter fighting, and MACBETH *is slain*

5:9   *Retreat and flourish. Enter, with drums and colours,*
              MALCOLM, SIWARD, ROSS, THANES, *and* SOLDIERS

MALCOLM   I would the friends we miss were safe arrived.

SIWARD   Some must go off; and yet, by these I see,
          So great a day as this is cheaply bought.

MALCOLM   Macduff is missing, and your noble son.

ROSS   Your son, my lord, has paid a soldier's debt.   5
          He only lived but till he was a man,
          The which no sooner had his prowess confirmed
          In the unshrinking station where he fought,
          But like a man he died.

SIWARD   Then he is dead?

ROSS   Ay, and brought off the field. Your cause of sorrow   10
          Must not be measured by his worth, for then
          It hath no end.

SIWARD   Had he his hurts before?

ROSS   Ay, on the front.

SIWARD   Why then, God's soldier be he.
          Had I as many sons as I have hairs,
          I would not wish them to a fairer death.   15

135

16 *his knell is knolled* This seems a callous comment but the boy's father is proud of him.

20 *stands* implies the head is on a pole standing on the stage

22 *compassed with thy kingdom's pearl* surrounded by the nobles of Scotland

29 *earls* this was a new rank of nobility created especially for this occasion

32 *exiled friends* for example, Donalbain

When Malcom's army shout **Hail, King of Scotland**, could Macbeth's head fall off its pole and shock them all for a second or two? Could Fleance appear at the side of the stage, watching quietly? Or is this simply a celebration of good having triumphed over evil?

This is the second king to die. Our emotions about the two deaths are very different. Compare them.

There are words here which echo the descriptions of the first battle (Act 1 Scene 2).

The two armies met. Young Siward found Macbeth, fought with him and was killed by him. Macduff challenged Macbeth and finally killed him. The victorious army then gathered together and Macduff brought in Macbeth's head. Malcolm was hailed as King of Scotland and he promised to reward the thanes who had fought with him. He invited them to his coronation.

And so his knell is knolled.

MALCOLM   He's worth more sorrow,
And that I'll spend for him.

SIWARD   He's worth no more.
They say he parted well and paid his score;
And so God be with him! Here comes newer comfort.

Re-enter **MACDUFF**, *with* **MACBETH'S** *head*

MACDUFF   Hail, King! For so thou art. Behold, where stands   20
Th' usurper's cursèd head. The time is free.
I see thee compassed with thy kingdom's pearl,
That speak my salutation in their minds;
Whose voices I desire aloud with mine:
Hail, King of Scotland!

ALL   Hail, King of Scotland!   25

                                        [*Flourish*

MALCOLM   We shall not spend a large expense of time
Before we reckon with your several loves,
And make us even with you. My thanes and kinsmen,
Henceforth be earls, the first that ever Scotland
In such an honour named. What's more to do,   30
Which would be planted newly with the time –
As calling home our exiled friends abroad
That fled the snares of watchful tyranny,
Producing forth the cruel ministers
Of this dead butcher and his fiend-like queen,   35
Who, as 'tis thought, by self and violent hands
Took off her life – this, and what needful else
That calls upon us, by the grace of Grace,
We will perform in measure, time, and place.
So thanks to all at once, and to each one,   40
Whom we invite to see us crowned at Scone.

                                        [*Flourish. Exeunt*

List of other titles in this series:

NT Shakespeare: Henry IV Part One
Lawrence Green
0-7487-6960-9

NT Shakespeare: Henry IV Part One Teacher Resource Book
Lawrence Green
0-7487-6968-4

NT Shakespeare: Julius Caesar
Mark Morris
0-7487-6959-5

NT Shakespeare: Julius Caesar Teacher Resource Book
Mark Morris
0-7487-6967-6

NT Shakespeare: Macbeth Teacher Resource Book
Dinah Jurksaitis
0-7487-6961-7

NT Shakespeare: The Merchant of Venice
Tony Farrell
0-7487-6957-9

NT Shakespeare: The Merchant of Venice Teacher Resource book
Tony Farrell
0-7487-6963-3

NT Shakespeare: Romeo and Juliet
Duncan Beal
0-7487-6956-0

NT Shakespeare: Romeo and Juliet Teacher Resource Book
Duncan Beal
0-7487-6962-5

NT Shakespeare: The Tempest
David Stone
0-7487-6958-7

NT Shakespeare: The Tempest Teacher Resource Book
David Stone
0-7487-6965-X